ADVERTISING OUTDOORS WATCH THIS SPACE!

Not all outdoor signs are billboards. Nor are the amenities that the outdoor contractors provide used uniformly. As this Miami charity says, 'When you're homeless you see the world differently.' The Miami Rescue Mission, USA 1996, Agency: Crispin & Porter.

ADVERTISING OUTDOORS WATCH THIS SPACE! DAVID BERNSTEIN

Everybody knows that we are living in the information age. Technology propels us further down this super-charged highway, and computers hasten our exchange of knowledge at a pace that leaves many of us breathless. Well, who would have believed that in this internalized technological age the oldest form of outdoor information exchange, the poster, would still be one of the most popular? What then makes it such a unique form of advertising?

The answer to that question lies in the way the medium is consumed. On the public highway, or from a passing car, bus or train, it is generally viewed in a split second. Our attention is snapped from its purpose by a moment's distraction. This is the poster's fate. But that very fate gives it its potency, its graphic language and powerful simplicity. Advertising at best is an interruption in our daily routine; and we don't directly pay for it or generally ask for it. We do, however, tolerate it and therefore make it work hard to capture our attention. The skill of advertising is to reduce; to take a complicated message and distil it down to a simple thought that is both informative and memorable. The message must open out inside our heads, not on the space in which it appears. And of course, the faster an idea penetrates your consciousness the greater its potential impact. The poster by definition is limited to very few words and simple images; but, and here is the skill, it is the clever juxtaposition of those two elements that gives the medium its power. The wonder of advertising is how so little can say so much: that is its true creative mission.

The poster then, is the medium where the ultimate skills of advertising come into play; that is what makes it so fascinating and so challenging. As media in general fragments, chasing smaller and smaller audiences — twenty television channels today, two hundred tomorrow — more people in more countries experience the power of the advertised message through posters — and other outdoor advertising opportunities, from bus-sides to petrol pump handles — than by any other means. The poster remains the only medium that is seen, potentially, by everyone. Good posters have the power to capture the nation's attention, which is perhaps why political parties still rely so heavily on them.

This book is a wonderful record of the achievement of the outdoor advertising industry from its earliest recorded manifestations to today's innovative developments. The question that remains throughout this evolution, however, is the same: is it art or is it just commerce? From Toulouse-Lautrec to Wonderbra, we experience the unfolding genius of the poster and its creators. Advertising is for some the art gallery of the high street, whilst for others it becomes the eyesore on the highway. Posters prompt controversy, employ persuasion and provide information. No city street would be complete without them.

John Hegarty
Bartle Bogle Hegarty

A. GAMES.

Dedicated to the memory of Abram Games (1914–96).
'We attend because we are momentarily baffled and thus we are ready to seek for the message which we will remember all the better for having discovered it in such a flash of recognition.'
EH Gombrich, foreword to exhibition catalogue, 'Abram Games, 60 Years of Design', exhibition sponsored by the Financial Times.

uinness

GA/P1/2270

PRINTED BY MILLS & ROCKLEYS (PRODUCTION) LTD IPSWICH

Contents

Calvin Klein, UK, 1996.

Introduction

This is a book about the last great universal advertising medium: outdoor – as it is known in the UK; in the USA it is more properly referred to as 'Out-of-home'.

It's a book about the advertising you encounter when you close your front door – from the outside. On the street, from a bus, *in* a bus, ditto train and trolley, ditto car and cab, or waiting for any of them. It's on highways, at supermarkets, sports grounds, airports. Up, down, all around, in the sky, underground...

Encounters may be distant and fleeting (though advertisers hope the message is neither). They are nearly always moving – you pass it, it passes you, the two of you move together. Sometimes you are both stationary – in a close encounter in an airport lounge.

By now you will have guessed that this is not an ordinary poster book. Nevertheless, you will find a few of your favourite classics, for it would be perverse not to include landmark designs. Nor is it a conventional history, though you should be able to pinpoint when things are happening. As for *where*, though the sources are chiefly the UK, Western Europe and North America, there is work here from every continent.

Nor is the book about art. Commercial art maybe. Art with a selling point. The poster was the location for trade and aesthetics to co-exist and occasionally mate. A happy medium. The same community of interest obtains today in commercially-funded street furniture, or contemporary public art created by eminent architects and designers.

This is a book about advertising; or, more specifically, *advertisements* – what they say, how they say it, where they say it and what they are meant to *do*. They are meant, eventually, to move brands. Many brands, in fact, were built on posters. Until recently, however, brand advertising was no more than reinforced by the use of the outdoor medium. But today attitudes are changing.

Outdoor meets the new millennium in bullish mood. There are new structures, new technologies, new advertisers, and new partners, such as local authorities. There is renewed belief in the importance of its role, central to a brand's communication. Could it represent bedrock in an age of fragmentation? Could that be what is gaining it market share in many European countries, fuelling a modest boom in North America and driving expansion in the Far East? Or is it the beautiful irony that its fundamental strengths have never been as necessary as in the contemporary frenetic scene? Exactly what those strengths are this volume tries to convey.

My thanks are duly and inadequately registered under 'Acknowledgements'. But there are echoes from everywhere. As Andy Warhol said, 'Everybody's influenced by everybody'.[1]

Art and advertising

Advertising began outdoors.

The earliest outdoor messages were probably inscriptions on Egyptian monuments. There is a quasi-commercial message on papyrus in the Louvre from 146 BC concerning the escape of two slaves from Alexandria and the offer of a reward. There were proclamations on tablets in Greece and tablets on walls in Rome. Signs in Rome would indicate items for sale or services performed. A bush meant a tavern, a goat a dairy, a knife a cutler. There were early versions of theatrical posters.

Town criers would summon crowds. Heraldic signs would convey messages of sorts. Proclamations were announced from the authorities' high walls or town squares.

Written proclamations survive from twelfth-century France. In late twentieth-century France a counter-terrorism proclamation bestrides the pavements of Paris. From billboards Singaporeans are besieged by their government to smile.

The first printed handbill was arguably one produced by William Caxton around 1477, a set of rules for the clergy during the Easter festival. Handbills were affixed to the doors of churches in Holland and Germany. In 1517 Martin Luther began the Reformation with ninety-six theses nailed to a church door.

Placards adorned modest sixteenth-century Dutch interiors – downmarket equivalents of oil paintings – and, as contemporary art shows,

Post A Note*

Post: 'to stick up on a post, fence or a board, door, wall, hoarding, etc.; to announce by placard.'

Post: 'to supply with news or the latest information'.(*Chambers*) For an explanation of poster sizes see Appendix, page 225.

* with apologies to 3M

Early nineteenth-century Parisian handbills. Black and white was restricted to official announcements long after the advent of colour printing.

specific bills were affixed to exteriors to indicate items for sale or services performed. Posted bills printed individually were the forerunners of posters: handbills printed *en masse* were the forerunners of newspapers.

In the sixteenth and seventeenth centuries Church and State held the monopoly of the earliest posters. Printed notices announced decrees, public events, meetings and, eventually, entertainments. Doctors were allowed to proclaim their skills, recruiters to attract the brave and gullible. Illustrations began to adorn and augment the text. Vignettes grew in size.

According to historian Frank Presbrey, the first hoarding for commercial advertising appeared in 1740 when 'a London clothing merchant asked the town crier's permission to place his shop bill alongside the official proclamations, with the result that the city council established a fee for announcements.'[1]

In France a law of 1791 allowed private individuals to put up posters, but they had to use coloured paper. Black and white was reserved for the authorities.

Commercial persuasion was an open-air activity and remained almost exclusively so until newspapers (their tax removed) became affordable to all and literacy became the rule rather than the exception. Though engraving and woodcuts relieved the largely textual letterpress form of posted announcements, it was not until booksellers began to place enlarged book illustrations in their windows that vibrant images adorned the streets.

A typical 1930s London street scene. The most appealing promise belongs to one of the stage shows.

From the earliest days of steam, railways and posters were closely associated. Stations and tracks provided sites, as this mid-nineteenth-century painting of Paddington shows. Soon after, *railways themselves advertised their services and destinations on hoardings.*

The triumph of the poster lay in the move of the image to centre stage, in image as message. Aloys Senefelder, a Czech, had invented lithography in 1798. It is based on the principle that water and grease do not mix. Draw a design on the fine, porous stone with an ink containing grease. Wet with water. Brush with ordinary ink – and the ink remains only on the design. Press paper on the stone and the design is reproduced. Sixty years later large formats and massive print runs were possible.

Jules Chéret drew his designs directly on to soft limestone slabs, one for each colour: the more stones the fuller the range of colours. Chéret settled on printing three or four colours with strong outlines.

Here was a creative medium in its own right – designs were made

on it and for it (rather than using lithography as a conduit for other art forms). And here was an artist who appreciated the medium's potential and demands.

Chéret lived in Paris, the world centre of modern art, and was alive to influences such as the Japanese coloured woodblock – simple, flat colours with unnecessary detail eliminated; the nineteenth-century tradition of popular illustration; the colours of Turner; the manner of Watteau (Manet dubbed him 'the Watteau of the street'[2]); and, of course, the intensity of Impressionism. Is it a coincidence that Impressionism and posters were born at the same time?

Chéret had worked in London for Rimmel for whom he designed lithographic showcards. His earliest posters were figurative compositions

14 *A poster for the man who made it all possible, on the centenary of his birth. Victoria and Albert Museum, London, 1971.*

Jules Chéret, L'Etendard Français, France, c1888.

Garish yellow and vermilion, promiscuous ladies and movement … the hallmarks of Jules Chéret. Vin Mariani, France, 1894.

mostly for theatres and publications. Gaiety, movement and joyousness are its hallmarks.

Henri de Toulouse-Lautrec was more down to earth. He referred to Chéret's suppression of black. That was understandable he said, but 'we have re-integrated it'. He did more, of course – with caricature, distortion, surprising juxtaposition. Chéret usually left lettering to another hand whereas Toulouse-Lautrec tried to integrate that too. And he made it legible.

Commercial advertisers also saw the medium's potential. They added their own demands which, to judge from Chéret's corpus of work, seems to have influenced him only slightly. Chéret was Chéret – a cult figure.

Charles Hiatt, a contemporary British critic and author, could not conceive of Paris without 'one of its most proclaimed characteristics'. A Chéret-less Paris would materially diminish its 'gaiety of aspect'. Hiatt refers to 'riots of colour, triumphant in their certainty of fascinating and bewildering the passer-by … One might as well attempt to ignore a fall of golden rain as to avoid stopping to look at them.'[3]

'Stopping to look' may have been the reaction hoped for by earlier message-makers but posters are predicated on movement. Nevertheless Paris, the birthplace of the poster, was blessed by boulevards which encouraged a more leisurely pace. Indeed, Dutch advertising historians explain Holland's late arrival on the outdoor scene by Amsterdam's absence of boulevards.[4]

A remarkable achievement. Over thirty words of information co-ordinated by the brand. Singer, France, c1880.

Henri de Toulouse-Lautrec developed Chéret's style, reintegrating black and featuring people who belonged to, if not the real world, at least the demi-monde. Henri de Toulouse-Lautrec, book poster, France, 1892.

Alphonse Mucha, like Senefelder, a Czech. Art Nouveau intricacy and entrails. Less movement than Chéret but more involved with the brand name. Mucha, Salon des Cent, France, 1896.

Art – buy and large

*Melk, The Netherlands, 1990,
Agency: PPGH/ J Walter Thompson.*

*Makoto Saito, Alpha Cubic,
Japan, 1995.*

Julian Key, Pacha, Belgium, 1964.

*Edi Andrist, Nicole Boesch,
Honda Civic, Switzerland, 1992,
Agency: AEBI/BBDO.*

The earliest poster artists expressed themselves no differently in advertisement than they did on canvas: Chéret, Bonnard (arguably Impressionists) and Mucha (Art Nouveau) were themselves. Thereafter, poster artists were eclectic. The best of them – Cappiello and Savignac, for instance – chose the style appropriate to the task. Elsewhere in the book you can detect movements that designers appropriated: Art Deco (Cassandre), Expressionism (Hohlwein), Symbolism (Games, Carlu), Cubism (Ashley Havinden), Photomontage (Kauffer).

On these pages Surrealism, Op Art, Collage and Assemblage are called into service.

Herbert Leupin, Maryland,
Switzerland, 1956.

Benson & Hedges Special Filter, UK,
1977, Agency: CDP.

Bruno Munari, Campari, Italy, 1960.

HP Sauce, The Netherlands, 1996.

Chéret was awarded the Legion d'Honneur for 'creating a new branch of art by applying art to commercial and industrial printing'. Though he didn't make advertising's Hall of Fame, the industry owes him a large debt. He made possible a medium which remains the toughest challenge for advertising's creative people. He brought to the labours of commercial persuasion the discipline of art – which is the reverse of the normal practice. His style, however, bred few imitators. The simpler style of Aubrey Beardsley, who apparently signed six designs at most, had a far greater influence, especially in the USA. A critic wrote in 1901, 'Beardsley is nothing if not subtle. Chéret would be nothing if subtle.'[5]

Advertising is a bastard art in the middle of an inexact science. The process begins with a science of sorts: marketing, media planning and research into the activities of the marketplace and the minds and habits of consumers. From these investigations a brief is prepared, a task is set, a proposition written. The creative team takes over and turns the proposition into an idea which is meant to move potential consumers towards purchase. The idea is executed in the various media. Thereafter the inexact scientist checks the outcome.

The science is inexact since advertising concerns prediction and the influencing of human behaviour, a notoriously difficult activity. The outcome of tests with consumers in laboratory conditions or controlled test markets is rarely replicated in the real world.

Aubrey Beardsley's 'precise fantasy' (Herbert Read) is never more practical than in this seminal theatre poster. Beardsley, Avenue, UK, 1894.

The classic French Job cigarette poster originally designed by Chéret in 1895.

The divine Sarah endorsed many products. Jules Chéret, La Diaphane, France, 1890.

the artist's reputation is another matter. Here is Hiatt in 1895 bemoaning Chéret's sameness. 'If one sees a great quantity of Chéret's work, one becomes aware of a certain feeling of monotony. One can be satiated even at Chéret's gaiety and joyousness.'[8] Though Chéret designed over one thousand posters, the personality which is conveyed is rarely that of the individual brand but of Chéret. Contrast that with Abram Games's comment, 'when people tell me they've seen one of my posters, they remember the name of the brand.'[9]

'The central motif of all [Chéret's] work was a full-bosomed eternal Eve with a dazzling smile full of *joie de vivre*.'[10] Casas chose to show women in more restrained poses. Mucha too impressed his own style upon the product or personage. Indeed, much of the work of the famous artists concerned arts of other disciplines – literature, theatre, circus, music halls, cinema – rather than commercial brands. Sarah Bernhardt was an early subject for both Chéret and Mucha. Culture, albeit popular, was a useful bridge spanning art and poster art. American magazines used posters. *Harper's Monthly* had its in-house illustrator Edward Penfield. Others commissioned Will Bradley and Maxfield Parrish. All were influenced by Aubrey Beardsley who also designed theatre posters. It became chic to collect examples from the un-posted runs of certain designs. International poster exhibitions were held between 1893 and 1897 in Hamburg, London, Brussels, Dresden, Rheims and St Petersburg. Boston staged America's first poster exhibition in 1895.

Same model, same mood, similar pose, two different liquids. Jules Chéret, Pippermint, France, 1900 and Saxoleine oil, France, 1892.

Branding the additive. Abram Games, Shell, UK, late 1950s.

Edward Penfield, America's first major poster artist, designed the covers for Harper's *magazine for six years. Copies were made and the 'art poster' became a fashionable collectible. Simple but powerful*

tableaux, eschewing movement. Edward Penfield, Harper's *magazine, USA, 1898.*

Famed US artists such as Charles Dana Gibson and James Montgomery Flagg would be persuaded to design posters. Magazines in Paris and London were devoted to the new art.

But were advertisers? It would take the new century to mature before poster art fused its two components, became the means by which the product benefit could be conveyed rather than simply a grand appendage to a brand name and, occasionally, a slogan. Most advertisers were asking the wrong question – 'what can we do with art?' – rather than the challenging one, 'what can we do *through* art?'

Art enabled an advertiser to deck his product with features, often classical, to suggest importance or authority. The link between product and image was often arbitrary and the justification barely existed. An advertising term for this is 'borrowed interest', the problem with which is that *anyone* can borrow. And so we see, early on, the creation of stereotypes. Machines have superhuman powers, bicycles are ridden by gods, Chéret-style ladies diaphanously gowned, accompany virtually any product. Indeed, when Chéret appropriately illustrated the hair colorant Les Sirènes with three sirens one wonders if the brand name was invented to fit his style.

Art could also enhance the mood of the passer-by, enliven the street scene, decorate an otherwise drab environment. But unless it was also saying something about the brand, was the advertiser no more than a patron?

Though if the early poster artists were primitive admen (and probably

Toulouse-Lautrec was a cavalier cropper of heads (see also Divan Japonais, p 75). Strong branding – and an aptly named distributor. La Chaine Simpson, France, 1896.

A one-off by Edouard Manet – this bookseller's poster for a novel by Champfleury. France, 1868.

content to be) they were also pioneering craftsmen. They knew how to exploit the medium's size; to master scale with simplicity of tone, bright patches and flat masses of primary colour; to utilize the idioms of existing popular art as in fairgrounds and circuses with their powerful images and short and legible messages. They painted murals but without the mural's complexity. Movement was at the heart. Chéret and his like would catch it on the wing. And the passer-by could, in turn, catch the image as he passed. An impression of a product, a promise. It may be fanciful to regard the near-simultaneous birth of Impressionism and the poster as anything more than coincidence. However, they are linked by the out-of-doors. While landscapes had long been a subject for artists, painting (as opposed to sketching) had

rarely taken place in the open air until the invention of metal tube pigments in the 1840s which enabled the Impressionists to paint *in situ*. And it was the Impressionists who, in the words of Daniel Boorstin, 'made an art of the instantaneous'[11] and Claude Monet who showed how it could be done. Poster artists, like other painters of the period, appreciated to the full the nature of outdoors and what constraints it put on communication.

Though the 'real' artist had no constraint equivalent to the pressure from a commercial client, he nevertheless worked faster than his forebears. The Impressionist 'accelerated the pace of his art', according to Boorstin, in order to 'match the pace of modern life'. Or was it simply to catch the changing light? He had more in common with the traditional Chinese painter

An early example of Shell giving artists their head. Jean d'Ylen, Shell, UK, 1924.

Jules Chéret, Carnaval 1894, Théatre de l'Opéra, France, 1893.

Is beer really her drink? Alphonse Mucha, Bières de la Meuse, France, 1898.

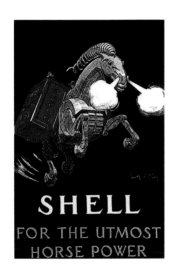

with his swift brush strokes than, say, Leonardo who returned again and again to his work on the wall of Milan cathedral (not so much a Last Supper as a running buffet).

Leonardo had defined the artist's task as 'saper videre'.[12] Conrad echoed this: the artist's job is 'to make you see'.[13] 'A work of art', said Paul Valéry, 'should teach us that we haven't seen what we're seeing'.[14] 'Art does not render the visible,' said Paul Klee, 'rather it *makes* visible.'[15] The poster enabled the public to see products. Products which consumers did not know were brought to their attention. In Europe the births of poster and brand were roughly contemporaneous. Products which were already consumed assumed further characteristics. Commodities were clothed with colour,

with image, and became brands. Ideally consumers were made to see the brand anew; to have their reasons for purchase reinforced.

Creativity – for whatever end – concerns the ability to see something anew, as if for the first time, and to articulate that insight. It is no use seeing in a new way if the mode of seeing cannot be communicated to another. The poster brought imagery to products and occasionally that imagery was coherent with the brand's attributes, i.e. physical make-up and performance. More frequently, as has been suggested, the imagery was bought wholesale.

Advertising is about ideas. The idea should arise from the proposition and be inextricably and, if possible, uniquely linked to it and to the brand. 'There is inherent drama in every product,' said Leo Burnett of the

24

In Casas's poster the brand character plays second fiddle to the statutory female. Ramón Casas, Monkey Aniseed, Spain, 1897.

Theophile Steinlen paints his daughter enjoying the product, with a cat (his trademark), two large, different versions of the company name, three letter forms … and yet it works! Compagnie Française, Switzerland, 1895.

Mucha stamps himself rather than the brand on this design. Alphonse Mucha, Nestlé Infant Food, France, 1897.

eponymous Chicago advertising agency. 'Our number one job is to dig for it and capitalize on it.'[16] (Not borrowed interest – burrowed interest.) Few early poster artists or advertising practitioners used their art to assist this process. Instead they added decoration to a brand, more or less appropriately and (with luck more than good management) exclusively.

A poster has to convey a message exclusive to the subject. Poster art is neither simply decorative nor pictorial. It is (as we shall see later) a fusion of words and image which needs must leap, reduce, arrest, impress and leave impressed in a few seconds a message upon an unsuspecting passer-by. This is not art to commune with, as in a gallery, but art with a definite job to do. As such, any critical judgement of the subject which omits to include among the criteria purpose and its achievement is unprofessional.

But then so is much allegedly professional criticism of advertising today. Advertising is still treated as an art form, entertainment medium or branch of show business. That it is, of course, all of these in addition should not diminish the prime importance of the commercial objective. If a commercial entertains then that can be regarded as a bonus. If the entertainment is a means of transforming a viewer into a consumer then the means are justified.

Similarly a poster may be (or become) art – again a bonus – but unless it is applied rather than pure, self-indulgence rules. Why does a *poster* hang on the wall? Why not a press ad? 'Posters make a contribution to culture,' says German-born Dutch designer Otto Treumann. 'That's a bonus, even

With a brand name like that the manufacturer knew the right artist for the job! Jules Chéret, L'eau des Sirènes, France, 1888.

Steinlen and even more cats. Theophile Steinlen, Quillot Frères, France, 1894.

The earliest advertisers believed in the power of repetition – even within one advertisement. Sometimes the identical image is repeated. More interestingly the three images differ slightly – by person or product variant or time of day.

Julius, Sarotti, Germany, 1915.

Ludwig Hohlwein, Tochtermann, Germany, c1910.

Jean Carlu, Spatenbrau, Germany, c1930.

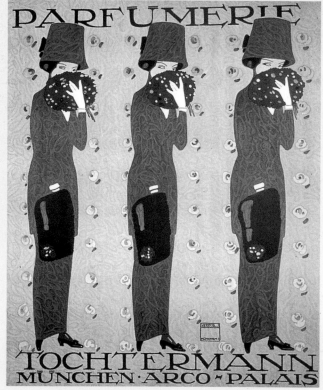

Coruba Rum, France, 1944.

Jean d'Ylen, Mik, France, 1921.

Eugène Vavasseur, Ripolin Paints,
France, c1900.

Eric de Coulon, Ancel Beer,
Switzerland, late 1920s.

Ashley Havinden, Eno's, UK, 1927,
Agency: WS Crawford.

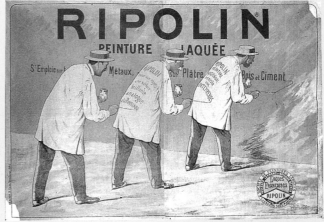

if it's not their original intention. But as graphic designers that's our aim. That's what I mean by a poster surpassing its ostensible purpose.'[17]

To whom is the poster artist or his latter-day equivalent responsible? To society, with whom he communicates and whose lot he can improve. To the client, without whom he goes hungry. To art which he plunders, hijacks, develops but never demeans. Is he an educator of the masses, forming a bridge to real art, making it accessible? Does he see himself as an artist-cum-guide in the art gallery of the street or subway? Again, any spin-off here, no matter how beneficial, is merely accidental. His job is not to bring the public closer to art but the consumer closer to the brand. Abram Games called the graphic designer, 'the middle man of communication'.[18]

What confuses the issue is that the principles and techniques of artist and bastard artist are identical. Each has to see anew and lend out his eyes. Each has to make the strange familiar or the familiar strange. Each has to evoke surprise.

As outdoor advertising developed, successive visual art movements were corralled into advertising – Art Nouveau, Cubism, Expressionism, Surrealism, Vorticism, Constructivism, Symbolism, Op Art, etc. Most of these forms were bastardized or trivialized. Some – with their simple lines, minimalism, vibrant colours, geometry or strange imagery were more appropriate to the advertising task than others. For example, the great monumental still-lifes and hymns to industrial shapes and vistas owe much to Cubism. Surrealism,

Shall I go cycling? What shall I wear? And what am I supposed to do with the mallet? A wavering cyclist by Alphonse Mucha. Waverley cycles, France, 1898.

Most of Casas's models confront the passer-by. Ramón Casas, Felix Murga, Spain, 1901.

Theophile Steinlen, Comiot Motorcycles, Switzerland, 1899.

by detaching the yoke of logic, allowed ordinary things to be seen afresh and, as with Symbolism, from several aspects at once: past and present could be portrayed and envisaged simultaneously.

The use of these various movements communicated another message: it said contemporary, the brand is in touch. Art Nouveau, though obviously linked to an idealized organic past, shouted 'new' and, depending on which country you came from, 'modern' (*le style moderne*), 'free' (*Liberty*), 'youth' (*Jugendstil*). These are still some of adland's favourite words. Symbolism, by developing the patterns and shapes of Art Nouveau and using classical or religious icons, allowed the poster artist to mask some basic human instincts with respectability, or at least, the artistic version. Cubism

permitted him to show more of an object (e.g. the product), from different viewpoints. Futurism (or 'the mechanism of design') suited some products more than others – cars, engines, planes and, especially, trains and liners.

Cassandre (born Adolphe Mouron), the pre-eminent artist of the mechanized, was one of the first poster artists to embrace the distinctiveness of his calling. The poster was not a display but 'an announcing machine', and should be distinguished from painting and theatrical backdrops.

Painting is an end in itself. The poster is only a means to an end, a means of communication between the dealer and the public, something like a telegraph. The poster designer plays the part of a telegraph

Carl Moos specialized in sport and fashion, not to mention simplicity of line, lack of detail, clever use of light and shade. Moos, Wagner, Germany, c1908.

Despite the brand name, this is an ad for an oil lamp battling against the arrival of electric light. Lucien Le Fèvre, Electricine, France, c1895.

The media's medium

Daily Mail, UK, 1930s.

*Shark Week, The Discovery Channel,
UK, 1996.*

Jazz FM, UK, 1996.

From the time of the first handbills other advertising media have used outdoor to promote themselves.

Magazines, newspapers, cinema and then television seem not to regard outdoor as a competitor for the advertiser's budget. For clearly, by appearing there themselves they implicitly endorse it.

If they entertain any qualms no doubt they are overwhelmed by the need to confront a mass audience on the move.

Radio 702, South Africa, 1996,
Agency: Partnership in Advertising.

LWT, UK, 1989,
Agency: The Creative Business.

Today, UK, 1991,
Agency: Yellowhammer.

Sonntags Blick, Switzerland, 1987,
Agency: Young & Rubicam.

official; he does not initiate the news, merely dispenses it. No one asks him for his opinion, he is only required to bring about a clear, good and exact connection.[19]

As advertising and competition advanced there was greater need for bigger sites and louder claims. Expressionism was called into service. Central was the content or plot, 'a skeleton that did not constitute a mirror image of reality but rather its hyperbole or occasionally its caricature'.[20] It was a language, paradoxically, of intolerance, disunity and fragmentation.

An alternative way of being heard amidst the tumult was to speak more quietly, to simplify the essentials. In England the Beggarstaffs, two painters working as a team, William Nicholson and James Pryde, depersonalized features, simplified elements and used clear, bold lettering. This economy was taken up by Lucian Bernhard and, to a lesser extent, by Ludwig Hohlwein in Germany. The poster consisted solely of the product and the name. But the tension between the two and the contrasting colours suffused the simplicity with tremendous force. In the 1920s the Swiss movement 'New Objectivity' turned objects into symbols and integrated the text (with uncluttered sans serif typeface) into the abstract but grid-locked design. It was coldly rational. Photography, seen to be truly objective, replaced 'art'. Photomontage, which originated in Berlin in the early Twenties, was a sort of borrowed objectivity though its objects were often bizarre as befits the Dadaist origins of its chief protagonist John Heartfield.

32 *Ludwig Hohlwein, Landauer Autos, Germany, c1900s.*

Two examples from Lucian Bernhard of the sach plakat or object poster – a million miles away from Chéret. Simply the product and the name. Lucian Bernhard, Bosch, Germany, 1914/1913.

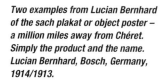

Surrealism served its turn on the hoardings. Reason takes a back seat. Images which defy logic, attract attention and emphasize brands and their benefits out of all proportion. The poster surprises by being not what it seems at first sight. And if pictorial problems take a little time to solve, well, the passer-by passes by more than once.

In such ways did 'real' art assist the advertiser in conveying the message. Whether the 'ism' is suitable (and often it ism't) or whether the art solution actually preceded the communication problem is difficult to say. Often the style of the poster simply reflected a contemporary fashion – as today a TV commercial may ape a feature film without apparent reason.

These movements had little effect on American poster design despite the early interest in European poster art. Their artists were concerned with portraying products clearly and with emphasis. Hyper-reality was the aim. Poster artists were largely anonymous but the products being presented were famous. Unlike their European counterparts, such as Cassandre and Charles Loupot, they were illustrators not designers. Although Bernhard and Jean Carlu emigrated to the US, they stayed true to their European roots.

There were also native exceptions. A discrete flowering occurred during the Depression producing what was called at the time, 'poster art more vital than this country has ever known'.[21] Artists rallied to the Federal Art Project sponsored by the Works Progress Administration (WPA). Between 1935 and 1943 two million posters were printed from 35,000 designs. To review the

Watercolours to promote ink colours – a dramatic departure for the artist. Ludwig Hohlwein, Pelikan, Germany, 1925.

Simplicity and visibility from the Beggarstaffs. Branding – but no product or promise. Kassama, UK, 1900.

Photomontage, angled lettering, an artist's drawing accessory (later used by Abram Games). Innovations from the American designer E McKnight Kauffer, Shell, UK, 1937.

small selection which survives is to be surprised by both the European influences and the little lasting effect the movement had on mainstream commercial poster design.

Paul Rand, as Stephen Bayley commented in his obituary notice, stood out from the 'mawkish realism' of the contemporary scene.[22] Before him Otis Shepard was known for the 'European style' of his Wrigley posters. He complained in 1931 of the 'pretty girl mania', a criticism repeated of more recent Japanese posters. Shepard thought advertising executives were 'magazine minded'. They transfer the page 'bodily to the poster panel. The realistic illustration … originally planned to be seen leisurely at close range becomes a poster board to be viewed on the run at a great distance'.[23]

Bernhard said of the American client, 'for him a visual idea is no idea. What he asks for is what he calls "human interest". If he gets it reinforced by a striking use of colour and good composition, so much the better.'[24] The majority of US boards of the period fit this bill. There are classics, of course, e.g. Chesterfield, Palmolive, Ford. But the norm is that of First Prize Ham where statement is all – and repeated – and involvement is nil.

It is difficult to believe that advertisers – even today – can rest their case on bland announcement. A major research study, conducted by the University of Alberta for Canadian outdoor company Mediacom, reinforced what many guessed, namely that, 'the kind of poster advertising that seems to make little or no impact had low memorability and was not deemed worthy

34

A double promise, the ad isn't a breakthrough though the board is. Clorox, USA, 1950s.

A press ad rather than a billboard. Some thirty words of text. An endorsement plus three 'benefits'. But the echoing of the logo in the main claim aids branding. Lucky Strike, USA, c1925.

Undemanding text and the required pretty girl – a common formula in the USA. JC Lyendecker, Chesterfield, USA, c1926.

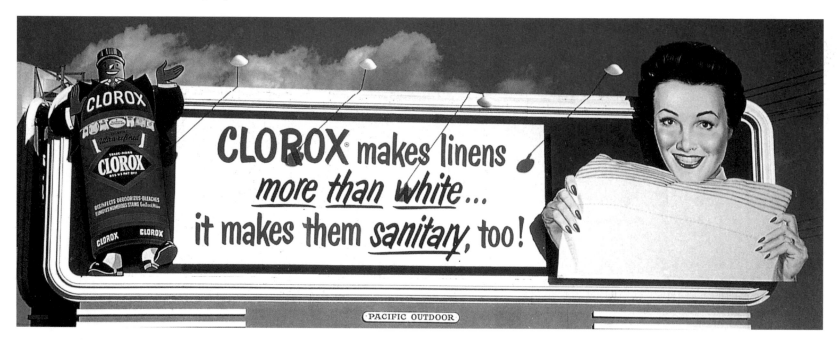

of consideration was the extremely literal type of poster, e.g. "The Best Cleaners In Town", "Introducing All-New Product X", "North America's Best Selling Scotch".'[25]

A British commentator in 1928 wrote of the US scene that, 'invariably the poster represents the man or woman using the goods advertised or containing a representation of the goods themselves'.[26] And, of course, if representation is what you want then photography is your medium. In the New York Art Directors' 23rd Annual Report (1941) one finds the following statement:

… the flat 'European' poster technique has been more and more discarded in favour of a three-dimensional rendering. Colour photography, photomontage and the airbrush have helped to streamline the American poster … Realistic-naturalistic posters are by far in the majority, with only an occasional modern, abstract or symbolic design here or there.

Ironically the best 'British' exponent of the European School from the late Twenties to the Forties was in fact born in the USA – Edward McKnight Kauffer. His contemporaries from Europe included Ashley Havinden, Tom Purvis, Tom Eckersley, Abram Games and FHK Henrion, plus émigrés from Nazi Europe such as Hans Schleger (Zero) and the partnership Lewitt-Him.

Immediately after the war a US poster designer wrote, 'We excel in technique, speed and fidelity of reproduction – especially in speed' and

A typical American board of the period. All claim and no involvement. First Prize Ham, USA, 1930.

Wit, branding and craftsmanship make the design stand out from other car billboards. Howard Scott, Ford, USA, 1931.

Otis Shepard was one of the few American graphic designers working in the 'European' style. Shepard, Wrigley, USA, 1932.

A few artists emigrated and brought the style with them. Lucian Bernhard, White Flash, USA, c1937.

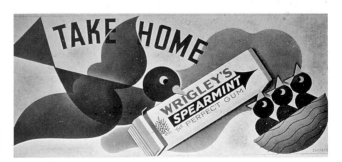

condemned the anecdotal illustration as insipid and unimaginative. It was sensational but 'crowded out by a mass of lettering'.[27]

By 1950 photography had assumed pride of place. The improved quality of magazine reproduction plus the reality of the new television image made the conventional poster image less and less relevant. The effect spread to the UK. As Ashley Havinden contributed to a *Times* supplement in 1964:

Graphic design – and indeed the art of the poster, as we used to know it – seem to have disappeared completely from the hoardings in favour of the 'blown-up' photograph. The appeal in advertising is no longer to the intuitive or unconscious part of the mind – but to the rational forefront of it, with the stress on cupidity.

If the left-brain – the logical, sequential, analytical – was dominating the Anglo-American scene, there was, however, ample evidence of right-brain ingenuity in France during the Fifties and Sixties.

Ideally, an advertising idea should be the solution to a specific marketing communication problem – the cream which comes to the surface of a particular bottle of milk. Alas, many advertising 'ideas' are artificial cream – they come from no one bottle of milk and belong to all and to none. Imitation of art, of other arts, and of the advertising business itself is rife. It feeds on advertising award festivals when the best, as determined by one's peers, are honoured, only to be ripped off by lesser talent the following year. There is a sad declension: yesterday's idea is today's technique is tomorrow's cliché.

36 *Leonetto Cappiello believed in surprise ('indispensable condition of all publicity'), visibility and brand attribution. Cappiello, Revel Umbrellas, France, 1922.*

But the poster artist who understands the task – a Cassandre, Savignac, Loupot, Leupin – stays true to the job in hand and is eclectic, employing the style, the technique, suited to the brand and to the communication strategy he has been set. Examine his work and the means never intrude or hide the end. You may detect an influence – Mondrian, Léger, Matisse, Magritte – but its appropriateness deflects any suggestion of self-indulgence or even homage. When Raymond Savignac shows us a car consisting mainly of a silhouetted driver and four tyres plus the Dunlop logo we don't say 'surreal' or mouth the name of a 'real' artist or ask why. We accept it and its own logic. Simplicity and synthesis were his driving forces. 'Il faut que j'arrive à l'essentiale', as he once said.[28] A poster artist so problem-oriented will not seek off-the-peg solutions. His job is to solve a communication problem by means of his art. It embraces analysis and expression.

Paul Rand defined the designer as a professional who tempers the instinct of the artist with the functional requirements of advertising. The designer's role is to 'restate his problem in terms of ideas, pictures, forms and shapes. He unifies, simplifies, eliminates superfluities. He … extracts from his material by association and analogy.'[29]

A graphic designer can choose to be simply a decorator, an augmenter of other people's solutions, making a personal and eclectic selection from Pop, Op, cartoon, etc. Sometimes the brief asks no more of him, as when the role of the poster is relegated to that of a support medium and the task

The Philishave razor has a circular head. That determines the design.
FHK Henrion, Philishave, UK, 1955.

Text at the heart of the message.
FHK Henrion, Super National Benzole, UK, 1960.

LE VERRE
TRIPLEX
S'ÉTOILE MAIS N'ÉCLATE PAS

to create (if that is the word) echoes.

Or the graphic designer can elect to return to the heart of the process. Hiatt got it right in 1895.

His first business is not to achieve a decoration, but to call the attention of the man in the street to the merits of an article ... the closest limits are set to his invention. It is not for him to do what he will but rather to do what he must.[30]

A future for the poster artist? Surely that can't happen without a renaissance in outdoor advertising. Is that likely? The writing is on the wall or, to be more exact, the images are out-of-doors.

Lettering was important for Cassandre. Here the T of Triplex infuses the design. AM Cassandre, Triplex, France, 1931.

Charles Loupot designed this character for a series of Valentine Paints. France, 1928.

Another Loupot. The same discipline and purity of style. Charles Loupot, Twinings, France, 1930.

The joke animal and its creator, Raymond Savignac, display perfect balance. Savignac, Cinzano, France, 1951.

Hervé Moran returns to the gipsy origin of the brand name. The product forms the sleeves and filters are evident in the shirt front. Moran, Gitanes, France, 1960.

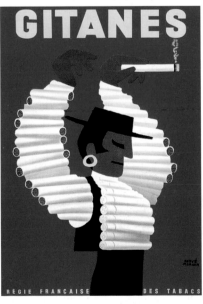

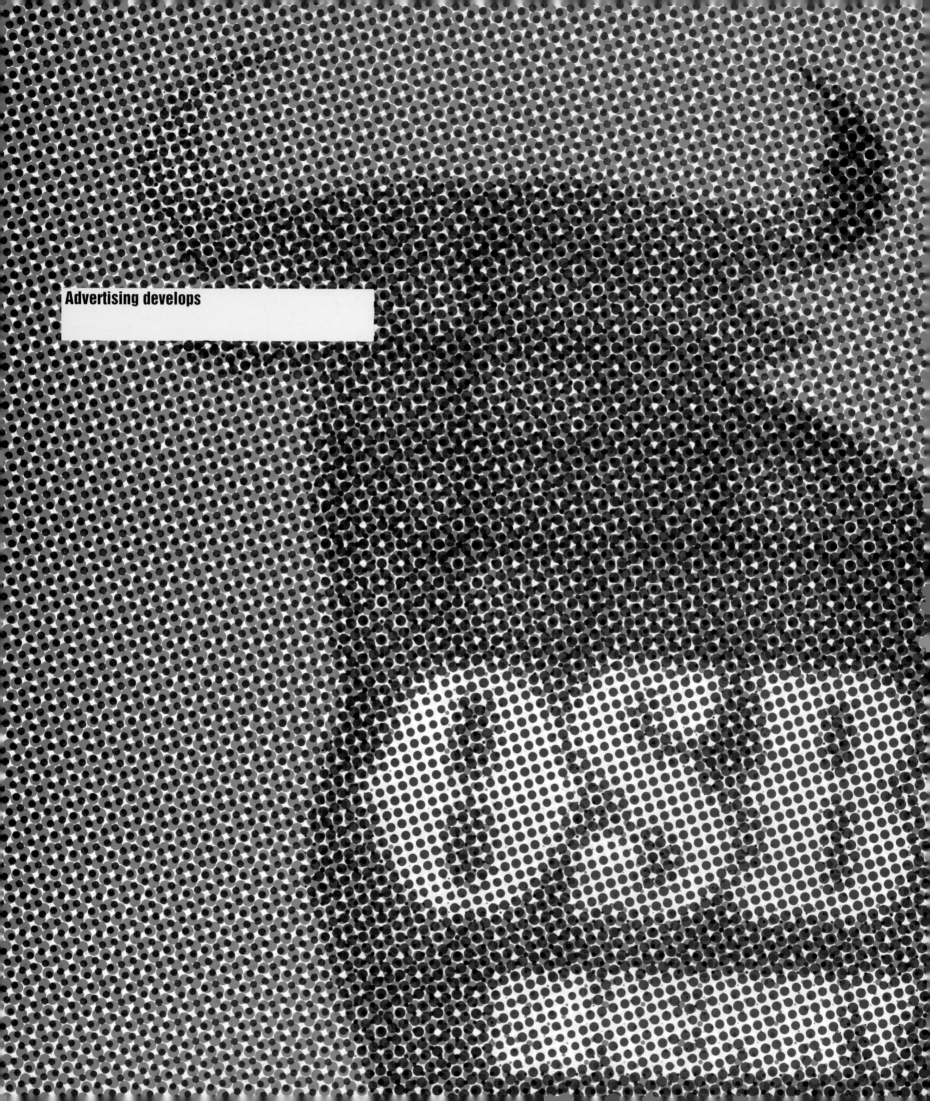

Advertising develops

Nathaniel Fowler, an American copywriter of the 1880s, said, 'All this poppycock advertising may look well and, like the sensational preacher, create a stir, but the question is, "Does it sell goods?"'[1]

In 1905 John E Kennedy defined advertising as 'salesmanship in print'.[2] Thirty years later two other American admen, Benton and Bowles, declared, 'it is not creative unless it sells'.

Undoubtedly, someone will stand up this year at a marketing conference and remind the audience that advertising is about selling. Advertising, since it uses the skills and techniques of art forms, is often mistaken for one. The pre-war assumption was that a copywriter actually had a half-finished novel in his bottom drawer, that the art director was a disappointed painter.

Post-war, the television commercial producer is preparing to become a Hollywood director.

The fact that some famous artists in these fields emerged as butterflies from the chrysalis of the ad agency should not delude us into regarding advertising as anything but a means to an end. Which end is not a new career but a sale. Raymond Savignac always recognized the commercial *raison d'être* and never wanted to become a painter.

Much contemporary advertising does appear remote from a sale. Can the perpetrators have forgotten its purpose or are they being clever – postmodern – in producing communication which acknowledges that the viewer is thoroughly advertising- and marketing-literate and therefore will

The headline tells us that the little girl is selling something, but there is no reason why we should purchase. An early example of 'umbrella' branding. Maggi, a Swiss design for the UK market, c1895.

not respond to an overt sales message but may, should he find the advertiser on his particular wavelength, accept the offering because it suits his lifestyle?

The postmodern theory seems to fit some of the obscure advertisements which hit the UK and other parts of Western Europe in the Nineties. But is it perhaps a *post facto* justification for a wrong-headed belief that advertising's first duty is to entertain?

Our early and unsophisticated advertiser had no delusions. An advertisement was meant to sell something. The job was not to decorate the media – pages or walls – but to plant a desire, accompanied by a reason to purchase the product. An 1880s US poster shows a pig with a human face. The product claim: 'Makes children and adults as fat as pigs.' The brand is appropriately named – 'Groves tasteless chill tonic'.

'Promise, large promise', said Doctor Johnson, 'is the soul of an advertisement'.[3] And, two hundred years later, the marketing man who forgets that is in trouble. Because, as Johnson may have known long before the likes of marketing guru Philip Kotler, people don't buy products, they buy satisfactions.

However, first things first, the advertiser must get across – and the viewer must recognize – the name of the brand. Branding arrived about the same time as the poster. Indeed, many famous brands, still alive, were launched on posters, Kodak, Wrigley, Heinz and Ivory Soap among them.

There's a promise! Grove's Chill Tonic, USA, c1880.

Before there were brands there were commodities. The grocer would stock barrels of biscuits and boxes of tea, pack and wrap them for each individual shopper. But if he had his name over the shop, why not also on the product? However, if he sold products which he did not actually make, he soon found that the manufacturer naturally was also trying to find a way of identifying himself with the end product.

Branding is essentially that – a means of identification. The term originates with the branding of cattle in the USA. It marked – literally – ownership. There is a story of one rancher who chose *not* to mark his cattle. So when any unbranded steer was found he could claim it as his. The rancher's name was Maverick – hence the term.

Branding has implications. When the maker puts his name on a packet he is also putting his name on the line. His reputation rides with every sale. The consumer knows whom to praise, whom to recommend to a friend, whom to complain to. A brand name conveys both memory – of past satisfaction – and *promise* of future satisfaction.

Early advertisers were in no doubt as to the importance of establishing the brand name – and had few qualms about the size of the name or logo. Posters afforded scale. Look at an old photograph or illustration of a hoarding – the brand names shout out. Singer, Coca-Cola, Sapolio, Quaker, Ivory in the USA. Bovril, Oxo, Colman, Beechams, Pears in the UK. Nestlé, Job, Michelin, Ripolin, Menier in France.

44

An 'object poster' from Julius Gipkens. Strong branding – and the promise is in the coloured background. Gipkens, Kaiser Brikettes, Germany, 1913.

Three promises but, above all, it floats. Ivory Soap, USA, c1898.

Terrific branding and use of colour. Note how artist Julius Klinger gets a vertical palm tree into a horizontal format. Klinger, Palm Cigars, Germany, 1906.

The brand name was more important than the descriptor (e.g. breakfast food) since a descriptor may fit competing brands. A brand is distinctive. Ivory said 'soap' but did not specify the type of soap. It mentioned how pure it was but stressed the unique fact that 'It floats' (the result incidentally of a rogue batch of product which Procter & Gamble subsequently duplicated).

A descriptor can limit the brand. Kodak subsumed rather than stated the word 'camera'. ('Take a Kodak with you', says an 1896 poster.) Coca-Cola is 'the real thing', or Coke with which 'things go better', but is never tied to a definition.

Bovril (once the name was changed from Johnston's Fluid Beef) was always to be advertised as Bovril. A 1903 showcard shows a lady and a jar and simply, 'Who says Bovril?' In 1938 the brand's advertising manager explained the advantage. Put the words 'beef tea' next to the brand and you remind the viewer of other beef teas. 'Today Bovril doesn't mean beef tea. Today it has come to mean "Bovril winter drink", "Bovril sandwiches", "Bovril in milk", "Bovril in the kitchen", "daily Bovril" etc.'[4] (Though that did not stop his American contemporaries from advertising it as 'the beverage beefsteak'.) Beef tea is a product: Bovril is a brand.

The earliest posters were basically announcements. The manufacturer would introduce his product and declare ownership: Smith's Tea – maybe with an injunction to purchase or an indication as to its place of availability. But when competition arrived – Brown's Tea – something more was

A promise of beef but no 'beef tea' descriptor. SH Benson, Bovril, UK, c1896.

Bovril generations later but hardly more politically correct. UK, 1981, Agency: Ogilvy & Mather.

Kodak said camera without saying camera. And camera soon said Kodak. Kodak, USA, 1910.

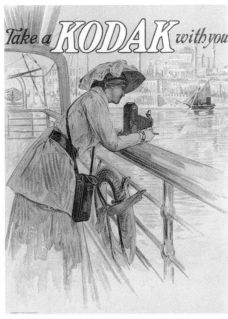

obviously needed. It was not sufficient to say merely what it was but why it was better or at least different. Branding does more than identify, it distinguishes. A brand has to be different in space though the same over time, i.e. different in real or perceived terms from the competition but deliver the same performance consistently.

Thus the next stage of development was Argument. Reasons for purchase. What makes the brand better and/or different.

A cocoa is 'the most nutritious'.

A soap 'will wash anything'.

A raincoat has 'quality, fit and finish'.

Sometimes the country of origin is sufficient justification – or an award won in international competition. But if the poster was capable of conveying only a few words of argument to buttress the claim, it could communicate a lot more by means of the image. To begin with, there was the image of the product itself – and the packaging – maybe fascinating because novel, maybe seen for the first time in colour and, with the improvement in printing processes, faithfully reproduced so that the viewer could be reassured when next encountering the pack on a shelf. Colour, size and glamour, exciting exotic subject matter could be brought in to aid the sale. So we get to the third stage: Association. Not just what it is and why it is better, but what it is like, where it is seen and who uses it. The advertising business had entered the world of *brand image* long before David Ogilvy popularized the term.[5]

46

The examples on this page are small posters or show cards for display in store or in the window.

An announcement. A family scene and the Peek Frean name.
Peek Frean & Co, UK, 1890s.

McCall and Stephen's biscuits offer an argument. McCall & Stephen, UK, 1890s.

Beware of being ripped off says Napoleon. He should know. Imperial French Coffee, UK, c1890.

Hovis not only provides a reason for purchase but associates the brand with the highest in the land. Hovis, UK, 1890s.

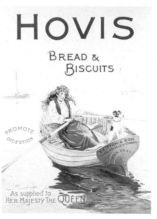

'Who uses it' suggests endorsement. Captain Scott actually *did* take Bovril on his polar journeys. But there is no recorded evidence that the Pope consumed it – though to be fair, the ad does not actually make the claim: the observer, however, makes the connection.

Similarly, in jubilee year, Queen Victoria appears to be endorsing a breakfast cereal. The words 'Ask for Golfer Oats' are next to her head. Beneath it is the pack. Beneath that 'The Two Safeguards of the Constitution'. Legislation to stop implied royal endorsement did not arrive till the 1930s.

Uncle Sam, a couple of years earlier, stands by a monster pack of Wheatlet, 'a delicate, delicious, breakfast food', offering it to a queue of eager foreigners. President Grover Cleveland was featured giving an unauthorized testimonial for Schlitz beer. Bismarck was depicted in Japanese posters for medical products. Britannia was rushed off her feet advertising metal polish, soap, biscuits, toothpaste, bacon and Harrogate ('Britain's Health Resort'). She rode a bicycle. As did John Bull who was also associated with lung tonic, Worcester sauce, ginger ale and at least four competing brands of cocoa.

Mythical figures, Wagnerian heroes, gods, demons … all were freely used by early poster advertisers. Sometimes ordinary people were imbued with superhuman powers. The Cosmos bicycle allows a lady to fly. The 'world's most beautiful child' owes it all to Virol. Beautiful women have been

Advertisers appropriated monarchy, heroes and sportsmen without permission, let alone payment, to invest brands with values outside the product. Golfer, UK, 1897.

The little girl holds an enamel advertising sign. An early example of ads featuring ads. Firmin Bouisset, Maggi, Switzerland, 1892.

associating with brands since posters began. It doesn't matter that we don't know their names or claims to fame. Mystery is part of the enchantment. All we are told is that, 'On her travels she uses Wells Fargo checks'.

Mucha and Chéret realized the importance of association – or maybe that is what they enjoyed portraying. The design could be allusive. Chéret, in advertising an oil lamp, believed that the poster 'would not dwell on the product'. But should it not dwell on something related, relevant to the product? How relevant is the scene depicted, the situation in which the brand is found? Often the choice seems arbitrary, not to say clichéd. Occasionally, however, the scene is distinctive. The viewer is intrigued. Instead of still life the poster echoes Victorian narrative painting.

See for example the Rowntree's Elect Cocoa poster. Who is the man in the bowler hat and skates – and what exactly is his relationship with the lady? 'Southend by District Railway' could almost be the title of a play, a thriller perhaps. Again, what exactly is the lady doing? There is a hint of mystery, too, about another lady and a train in Caillers' chocolate poster. Why *did* Jones stay late at the office? Was it simply to enjoy a pipe of Ogden's Midnight Flake?

An Ivory soap poster of 1890 features some twenty men, mostly stripped to the waist, washing from oak barrels of water on which floats the brand. They are standing outside a smoking foundry. One man, also smoking, sits, dressed, on a box of the brand.

48 *Each of these posters invites participation by the viewer. Who are these people? What exactly is going on? And while we question, the brand names register.*

Wells Fargo, USA, 1917.

Potage, Maggi, France, 1890s.

Rowntree's Elect Cocoa, UK, 1899, Agency: SH Benson.

Watts, Southend by District Railway, UK, 1912.

Ney, Caillers, UK, 1901.

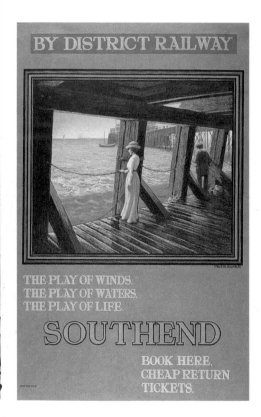

Much of the brand imagery of the period owed more to the artist than to the brand itself. There was a danger of similarity rather than distinctiveness between competing brands in the same category and non-competing brands in different categories. At that time in the UK, however, the prevailing view was that, 'the chief, if not the sole, effect of posters is to familiarize the public with the name: it is the dreary drip of constant iteration.'[6]

In France, Cassandre saw that the poster had ceased to be a display: the 'announcing machine' was a part of the repetitive process of mass-communication.[7]

Repetition, nevertheless, is an important and worthy advertising tactic. It reminds people of the product's existence. It gets across the name of a new product. Outdoor advertising has had many successes in the launch period of recent brands. Perhaps the most striking recent exemplars are the Japanese and Korean companies in Europe who chose posters, airport and perimeter advertising at sports arenas to blazon their names, to ensure familiarity before ever revealing what it was they actually made.

This three-stage 'history' of advertising development – Announcement, Argument, Association – may seem simplistic. For this I make no excuse, nor do I want to suggest that a poster could only succeed in tackling one element. Indeed, there is usually a need for all three to co-exist.

However, it is useful to decide where priorities lie. They may differ according to the type of product. A serious product may seek to eschew

Ogden's, UK, 1909.

A narrative painting with the brand cleverly integrated. Ivory Soap, USA, c1890.

The original 'object poster'. It won a competition and launched Bernhard's career. But by the mid-1920s his contemporaries would dismiss the technique as simplistic. Lucian Bernhard, Stiller, Germany, c1905.

Fish, which cannot live outdoors, populate billboards.

Though, unlike birds, beasts and insects, they have no vocal language, they are a *lingua franca*.

Is the fish an icon, a convenient recognizable symbol?

Or something deep in a collective unconscious, a cross-cultural representation of humanity?

On the other hand *affiche* is the French for poster.

Luigi del Medico, *Schweppes*, Switzerland, 1992, Agency: Farner Publicis FCB.

In support of US protection against the Soviets. Tashi Kono, political poster, Japan, 1953.

Select Appointments, UK, 1980s, Agency: Mavity Gilmore Jaume FCA.

Wrangler Jeans, USA, 1995, Agency: The Martin Agency.

Koichi Sato, New Music Media concert poster, Japan, 1974.

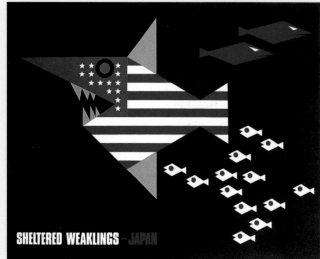

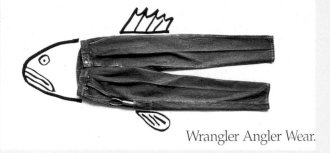

Kyösti Varis, Savon Sanomat
Newspaper, Finland, 1970.

Electricity Council, UK, 1989, Agency:
BSB Dorland.

Celestino Piatti, Rolex, Switzerland,
1975.

Barrons, USA, 1995.

J Nunney, Ministry of Agriculture and
Fisheries, UK, 1930.

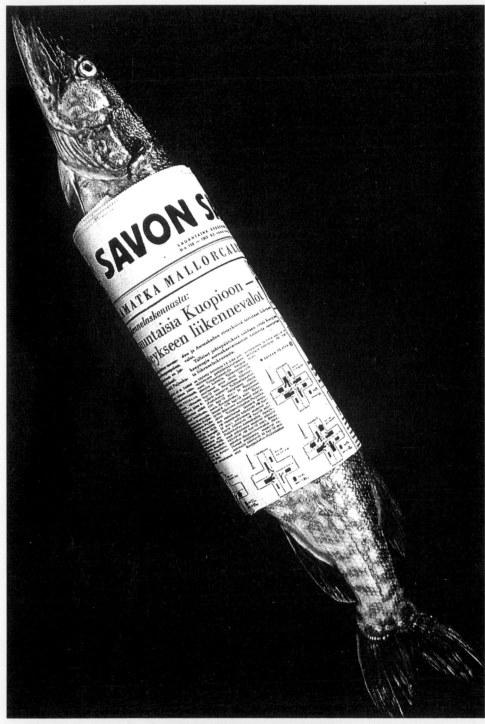

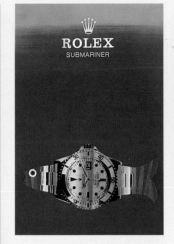

ELECTRIC FAN OVENS WON'T LET FLAVOURS GET MIXED UP.

GIVE THEM FISH
it's so easily digested

EAT MORE FISH

association and rest its case on plain fact. But facts once presented are never plain. The choice of typeface, colour, size and relationship of elements are all conveying 'associational' values even in the most factual advertisement. What could be more basic than Bernhard's designs for Priester and Stiller – the product and the brand name?

Argument was important in Holland and, according to a Dutch commentator, was another factor delaying the development of national poster art. 'People wanted to be convinced of the soundness of the quality of the goods being offered and they wanted to be convinced by argument … The willingness to accept visual arguments with the same readiness as textual was certainly lacking.'[8]

Early Dutch poster professionals debated the merits of announcement and argument. As a commentator in a trade paper wrote, 'There are two things an ad can be. It can either be a simple piece of information or it can be a shout … There is no need to shout out the truth because it can be stated quietly without having to be over-emphasized.'[9]

This implies that a lie has to be shouted. Of course many advertisers make up in decibels what the brand lacks in difference. But distinctiveness can reside in style, in the manner of the communication.

A contemporary Dutch poster artist, in a riposte to the sentiment of the previous extract, responded that, 'if the artist is genuine even his shouting is beautiful'.[10]

52 *A poster is the pictorial equivalent of a shout.* L'Equipe *sports paper, France, 1980s.*

The three As – Announcement, Argument, Association – form a practical checklist to employ if your job is to plan and evaluate advertising. It is quite a good game to play when watching television or if you are stuck in a traffic jam near a poster site. Procter & Gamble incidentally used to adopt a similar holy trinity when briefing and judging advertisements – Benefit, Reason Why, Tone of Voice.

The poster medium soon moved through all three stages. However, with the development of cheap newspapers (and universal literacy) argument was more fully accommodated in print. Initially, newspapers and magazines reached more people than urban posters. In the USA, for example, it was not until the growth of cars and the improvement of major roads that outdoor advertising became significant in small towns and in the countryside between, though barns, walls and railway rights of way were painted to attract travellers on trains.

As magazine reproduction improved, brand images could be carefully nurtured, the product features accurately detailed. Then with the development, first of radio, then of television, association could be exploited in the broadcast media.

And if Chéret introduced glamour, television also had all the trappings of showbusiness of which some members of the advertising industry craved to be part. Adbiz was born and advertising people aped their showbiz brothers and sisters with a gossipy trade press and awards festivals in all the

A billboard promoting outdoor advertising. Aepe, Mexico, 1995.

VALLA PROVOCACION

LAS VALLAS LLAMAN TU ATENCION   aepe

in-places. Means became ends. New theories of how advertising works arose – based on emotion rather than reason, and entertainment rather than product facts. And recently postmodernism has become the name of the game.

Not that all this was hedonistic or indeed non-productive. Great sales successes were achieved and well documented. Advertising effectiveness awards (i.e. based on the relationship between the ad and the sales achieved) proliferated, replacing, in professional esteem, the more cosy competitions judged by one's peers. However, in this fashion-conscious world imitation is still rife despite the fact that the strategy for an execution successful in one product category, may be totally unsuitable in another.

Today, although we may know more about how advertising works in particular instances, there is still no universal model. Moreover, there is greater realization that the holy grail will never be reached. So, in an environment where nothing is absolute, one philosopher's stone is as good as another's. It's still the bastard art in the middle of an inexact science, which I joined forty years ago. And because of this it still attracts many talented people who wish to crack the science or exploit the art.

Television, of course, offered more than the trappings. It delivered drama, movement, music, sound effects. It could convey a brand image on the first transmission of a launch commercial. Production values could reinforce an idea. Sometimes, alas, all the ad has are the production values and it takes

54 *Very strong suction. A vacuum*
cleaner demonstrates its strength.
AEG, The Netherlands, c1990.

a well-trained eye to separate production values from brand values.

In the face of television's dominance – and, in particular, the creative people's influential liking for the medium – outdoor advertising was generally relegated to a supporting role. And within agencies the designing of a poster was relegated to lesser, junior staff and poster origination (if that is the word) was tackled late and in haste.

For a decade in the UK at least, the poster served as a reminder of advertising in other media, generally television. Sometimes it was no more than a pack shot plus slogan (a throwback to the earliest posters). Sometimes it was a scene from the commercial with the end line. It is salutary to compare these with the best cinema posters which rarely used

stills from the film but instead endeavoured to capture the essence of the film by means of juxtaposition of stars and artifacts.

The advertising poster had a place in the advertiser's affections though not in his schedules. Outdoor had ceded pole position long ago to other media. Not universally, of course, and there are encouraging signs of renewal (see, 'The future'). But by and large the story of outdoor advertising has been one of a decreasing share of advertising expenditure. Outdoor is almost always seen as a support medium, less strategic than tactical, serving less to impact, intrigue and involve than to *remind*. Having said that, the real success stories are glorious exceptions to this rule.

The foregoing has described the situation in the UK, USA and most of

This Toyota board is a cute reminder of a television commercial. But to the innocent eye it is virtually meaningless. Toyota, UK, 1997, Agency: Saatchi & Saatchi.

This Evian ad can work as a TV ad – and communicate on its own. Evian, UK, 1996, Agency: Euro RSCG.

Europe. The French of course, as true begetters of the poster, guarded its traditions, encapsulating the brand's promise on the hoardings. This despite the vigour and ingenuity of much of French television advertising.

Outdoor's role today is not confined to reminder advertising. And even where it is, there are ways of doing it which exploit the medium rather than using it merely as non-moving versions of television. When advertising's creative teams become obsessed with the box the result is often a poster which betrays their obsession. Instead of taking the idea and reinterpreting it for the medium they try to re-present the commercial, making the inappropriateness of the execution only too apparent.

Instead of exploiting the strengths of outdoors (see 'The strengths of outdoor') they reveal not only the medium's limitations when asked to pretend to be something else, but their own lack of vision. They are, it should be stated, not alone in this. The outdoor medium has often looked over its shoulder at the box and endeavoured to do its own version of television outdoors. Movement is a perpetual fascination with the outdoor industry but while there is more sophistication today (see 'Beyond the billboard') the results are not entirely satisfactory. Tri-vision which allows three images to replace each other is, to my mind, far more successful when the images are discrete – i.e. for separate advertisers – and held for sufficient time to be seen as still, rather than as part of a moving spectacle. Similarly, moving signs are surely meant only for those locations where

56 *The board presumes the viewer knows this sung catchline from a credit card campaign. Access, UK, 1980s, Agency: GGT.*

people traditionally stand and stare rather than a busy highway.

A reminder poster need not reproduce the TV or press ad so much as be coherent with it. Clearly the message should be seen to be coming from the same source, to be conveying the same sales point, to be speaking with the same tone of voice. And if there is a campaign theme line then that should be displayed. Yet, despite all these caveats, there is still room for the idea to be expressed for and through the medium. The advertiser and agency have to weigh the advantages of having a universal campaign idea capable of identical execution in all media, against the benefit of exploiting each individual medium to the full. Inevitably there must be a trade-off.

Do you make the tremendous television commercial which will not work in other media? Or do you make a less thrilling commercial which is capable of extension into all other media? And if you decide on the former, what do you do in the other media? There is no universal rule. And what complicates the discussion is not simply the various strengths and possibilities of the competing media but the definition of the advertising idea. Ideas are notoriously hard to define. Try it out on any campaign you know. Are you defining the strategy or the idea? The idea or the execution? Is it the copy line or the image? Is it the even less tangible personality which is being conveyed? If television allows you to demonstrate, will a mere still photograph of the end result suffice – or a couple of side-by-side shots – as the outdoor board? Not all advertisers have the type of product or the

The first of two examples of using the brand name as a design element to convey a promise. Datsun, UK, early 1980s.

The mouth-cloying photograph works well with the question. An excellent made-for-the-medium variant of a TV campaign. California Fluid Milk Processor Board, USA, 1994, Agency: Goodby Silverstein & Partners.

The brand name used to convey a benefit. Amoco, USA, 1984, Agency: D'Arcy McManus Masius.

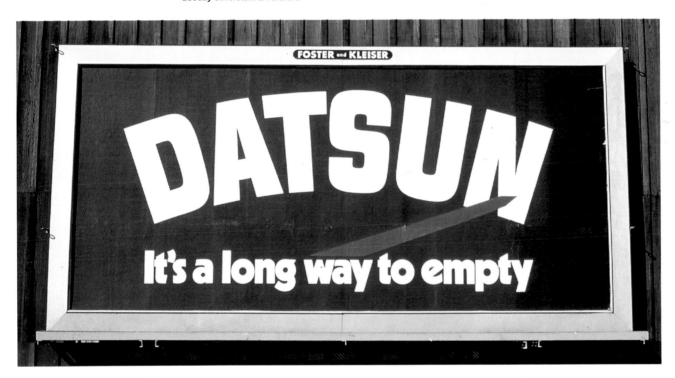

ingenuity of Araldite, in sticking a car to their hoarding. Yet, there are ways of depicting before-and-after without resorting to the obvious.

Though there is no golden rule concerning media choice, there is a simple fact that we shall explore later: if it works as a poster it will work anywhere. But, let's face it, outdoor is very largely used as a reminder medium (or, to put it another way, as a means of delaying the decay of the TV advertising) and there are creative as well as ordinary means of reminding – as these pages remind us. There are creative ways of using an image to provide a visual augmentation of a radio campaign. And by creative I mean what a J Walter Thompson writer, James Webb Young, described as, 'doing the unusual with the usual'.

What other parts can outdoor advertising play in the campaign?

To begin at the beginning – *announcement*. Announcements of public importance had traditionally taken place in the open air: the speech in the agora, the town crier, the royal decree on the balcony. The painted handbill announced a sale, an auction, an election. Today the poster's message may represent the first intimation of a new brand or a new version of an existing brand. It may, as with the Japanese, represent the arrival of a new company.

It may be difficult to assess the impact of posters when you can't be certain where or when or how you heard about a new brand. However, when you travel you may have the impact of outdoor dramatically proven. For instance, you go into a pharmacy to buy toothpaste, they don't stock

58 *A mould (and billboard) breaking campaign for Ciba Geigy's epoxy resin. Araldite, UK, 1982, Agency: FCO Univas.*

your favourite brand and/or the assistant recommends a domestic variety. Yesterday at home you may not have heard of it, yet today you feel you know the name. You probably saw it on a poster at, or on the drive from, the airport, or on a passing tram. Name registration is still important and, though some might argue that launch is only a preliminary phase in a brand's advertising career, it must be remembered that each day new people are (we hope) coming into the market. Hence the earlier comment that every advertisement should contain all three of the As.

Outdoor can be used simultaneously with other media to add impact or subsequently to extend the campaign. Outdoor can provide a shop window for brands denied a high street presence because the retail outlets are out of town – or for the retailers themselves.

Alternatively, the brand can tie in with the point of sale by occupying a site near the outlet or on the car or bus route to it. One of the problems besetting manufacturers of fast-moving consumer goods, particularly in foods, toiletries and washing products, is that their distributor is also a significant competitor. The retailer has developed a close relationship with the consumer, has the technology at point of sale to study purchasing patterns and has honed his or her marketing and advertising skills to compete at a professional level, pushing his or her own-name products, even stand-alone brands. Anything you can do – he/she says to the manufacturer – I can do better. And the manufacturer having nowhere else

A retail ad next to the store. Ribena, UK, 1997, Agency: Grey Advertising.

This Duty Free poster confronts all traffic entering Bahrain International Airport. The friendly alien holds a 20 dinar note. His legs are the concrete legs of the site. Bahrain, 1995, Agency: Gulf Advertising.

to go (unless he/she becomes a retailer or sets up a new distribution system) has to find a way of renewing and building on his or her relationship with the consumer. Outdoor provides a useful vehicle for communicating with consumers when they are in a buying mood. This need not be just a simple five-word reminder of a commercial. After all, a single site at eye level near a shopping precinct or at a bus stop can invite readership, even study.

Outdoor can reinforce brand advertising, not echoing it but underpinning it with the name of the company. The subject of corporate advertising is the company rather than individual brands. The core values of the company may be proclaimed. Alternatively, a selection of the company's brands is featured – what is known as 'umbrella branding'. Such a strategy may be necessary

when the advertising budget for lesser brands is relatively small. Moreover, advertising the company name can act as a means of reassurance when a new brand is introduced.

A potent advertising medium is sampling. Conventional advertising wisdom posits a linear progression from attitude to behaviour. Change (or reinforce) the consumer's attitude and that will trigger a change (or continuation) of behaviour. It is very logical, although the traffic is two-way. Behaviour also affects and effects attitude. Simply ask yourself which car ads particularly attract you (those for the one you drive perhaps?). So, initially, how can we bypass attitude and go straight to behaviour, thereby influencing attitude?

One of the earliest examples of Calvin Klein's large-scale advertising. Calvin Klein, USA, 1980s.

Impact plus involvement – in a location where people have time to read. Levi Strauss, USA, 1995, Agency: Harrod & Mirlin.

The first risk is not to have insurance. Europ Assistance, Belgium, 1996, Agency: Loewe Troost.

Marlboro, The Netherlands, 1996, Agency: Leo Burnett.

Sampling attempts to do just this. Despite Calvin Klein's huge expenditure on outdoor advertising, the sum is surpassed by his spend on scent strips in magazines. If the advertiser is so assured of his brand that he is convinced that one trial will convince the consumer, then giving it away – to the right people, of course – is a profitable route.

Outdoor may seem an unlikely medium for this. Nevertheless, it has scored some unusual successes. Nor need the product be given away. The outdoor structure can be used to offer sample size packs at a nominal price. So much for literal sampling – there is another variety. What we might call metaphorical sampling.

In a sense, an advertisement should be a sample of the brand.

The experience of consuming the advertisement should be a foretaste of the experience of consuming the brand itself. This could be summed up inadequately as 'what you see is what you get'. Coherence is crucial and (as discussed in 'Brand and Consumer') the brand must always act in character. That character has to suffuse the message, has to transform the words and image into something the passer-by can somehow sense. Bonnard's 'France Champagne' is the spirit of the drink. After seeing the idiosyncratic Guinness advertising you will hardly expect conventional beer. After participating in the mind game set by the *Economist* you will hope not to have your intelligence insulted when you read the magazine. The cheek of VW Beetle advertising is maintained the moment you turn the ignition key. The simple yet arrogant

A sample of the brand. Pierre Bonnard painted the lady sparkling amidst the bubbles. Bonnard, 'France Champagne', France, 1891.

clarity of Absolut vodka ads are confirmed in the glass and on the palate.

Outdoor advertising is a means of extending a national TV or press campaign to a locality. Location is one of the medium's main strengths. The advertiser knows where the consumer is at the moment of impact. With a little ingenuity the national campaign idea can be made location specific and thus move the brand and consumer closer together.

Finally, outdoor provides an opportunity for a company or brand to get itself talked about. This is known in the trade as a 'media multiplier' effect. An advertiser does something newsworthy on an outdoor site which attracts media interest (not without a little help from the advertiser's public relations team) and generates favourability or in some cases notoriety.

Benetton has aroused a mixture of reactions from admiration to disgust as its outspoken visualizations of topics of the day have hit the streets, becoming more and more provocative. This is association rather than announcement – and argument of another sort results.

Less provocative, but more related to the product, has been the Wonderbra campaign featuring a well-endowed lady who – if the tabloid press is to be believed – caused male drivers to crash their cars.

Levi's customized a bus shelter in London, replacing the seats with armchairs. Denim covered the armchairs. The press covered the story.

Sometimes the novelty or outrageousness of the image and message will be sufficient. At other times the use of the medium in a new way will

What began as a celebration of the unity of man across divisions of race and border, developed into a commentary on despair and tragedy. Was the campaign an expression of genuine concern by a compassionate company or cynical exploitation of human grief for commercial purposes? The jury is still out. A global campaign originated within Benetton under the guidance of creative director Oliviero Toscani. Benetton, Italy, mid-1980s to 1990s.

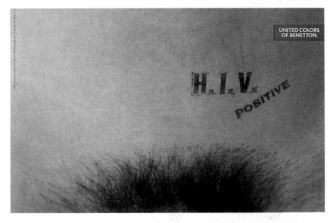

ABSOLUT BERLIN.

generate publicity. Then again (see 'Beyond the billboard') the medium itself will be novel so both the media owner and the brand are talked about.

When a creative team sits down to devise an ad campaign it needs to know if the task is to say something new or to say something in a new way. Usually it is the latter since breakthrough new products are rare. But a brand does not have to be new to make news. Nor does the medium. The column centimetres and broadcast coverage generated by outdoor innovation is a testament to the ability of both the advertiser and the medium constantly to refresh themselves, to make the familiar strange.

An international campaign built on identification with national locations. Being on the street helps a brand belong. Absolut, USA, 1988–93, Agency: TBWA Chiat/Day.

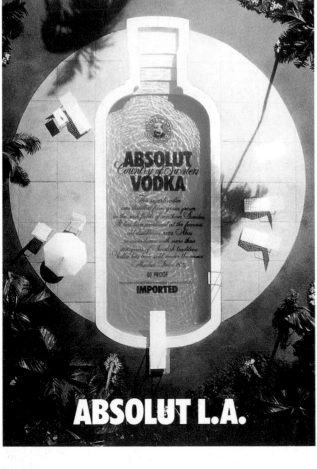

Poster rules

'orchestrated freely and largely into a massive scene of colour in order that the general pattern or design may be well and rhythmically mapped'. So said an early critic and art historian.[3] 'The poster must be more picture than matter', said another.[4]

It makes the designer more important than the writer. But – assuming they are not the same person – they have to work together. Savignac insisted that the text must be at the heart of the design – and most of his designs prove that both metaphorically and literally.

Bernard Villemot said, 'a good poster could be a telegram'.[5] If necessary, words should be included, provided they were incisive. But that does not allow the visual element to be any less spare. 'The less one shows the more one says', was Savignac's advice.[6] Prior to the colour lithograph posters were black and white printed notices. These were meant to be read. The very early poster artists assumed their efforts would be, if not studied, at least appreciated by stationary pedestrians. Such drama as the work contained is inherent rather than overt. It requires extracting from the scene depicted. It soon became apparent, though not universally, that complexity was inappropriate. A poster had to 'convey an idea rather than a story'.[7] Drama became melodrama. More obvious, more impactful. The decorative and delicately-hued vignette became a brightly coloured design. Textual content was reduced to headline or slogan. The design likewise became encapsulated. The aim was to condense the visual and pictorial information

Immediate relief from the worst headache. Raymond Savignac conveys it all in one vivid image, one word and the brand name. Savignac, Aspro, France, 1964.

Again Savignac communicates an important message. If safe holiday motoring depends on good tyres, why show the rest of the car? Savignac, Dunlop, France, 1960s.

into a single graphic 'punch'. Designers had their own words for this process and for the end results: 'The technique is economical and emphatic rather than artistic for the sake of being artistic. Similarly the colours are simple, underlying the theme.'[8] 'The design must be reduced to the simplicity of a traffic sign, eliminating all detail so that it becomes a kind of *visual shorthand*, easily recognized and remembered.'[9] 'My initial effort is always directed towards finding a symbol, a form or a trademark which will translate the subject of my poster as concisely as possible, and will also permit graphic interpretation of the greatest possible impact.'[10]

Not all British poster artists managed this mix of simplicity and impact. Two British critics felt the continentals did it more tellingly: 'The [German]

artist has been trained to limit himself to what he has to say, and to say that with all his might.'[11]

The poster is essentially compressed power. Abram Games compared it to a tightened spring which the viewer touches and so releases. The effect is immediate. An idea is communicated instantaneously.[12]

Simplicity is key. Achieving it is not simple. The physical format of outdoor and the environment in which it works, force the designer to be highly disciplined in order to succeed.

For the poster is like no other advertising medium. It is on its own. A poster is a poster – nothing else. Street furniture may serve other functions, but the poster has no other purpose. It has to make its own way in life,

70

The previous Dunlop design by
Savignac had tyres but no car ...
Dunlop tyres, UK, 1987,
Agency: Abbott Mead Vickers.

Simplicity and impact. A visual
pun communicating the Golf's
reliability. VW Golf, France, 1993,
Agency: DDB Needham.

whereas the print ad does not exist without the newspaper or magazine. The TV commercial does not exist without the programme which surrounds it.

The poster is pure advertising. It is naked. And naked, too, is the designer. A Swedish ad man, Kaj Hansson, calls the poster designer a stand-up comedian, making contact with an audience who may not want to listen, unsupported by fellow entertainers.[13] Make a mistake and it's public. Make a mistake in the press and it lasts as long as yesterday's newspaper. Make a mistake in television and it is lost in the torrent of communication but make a mistake on a hoarding and the error is public. The skeleton is out of the cupboard dangling above the highway with your name on it. Which of course is the downside of public communication: when you succeed you are noticed again and again. Though this brings in its wake the problem of wear-out. How long can the striking image stay aloft? If you employ surprise can the shift in perception demanded of the passer-by occur more than a few times before familiarity breeds invisibility? Can a joke bear repetition? Can the treatment support the message with the added value of character or style so that the viewer on revisiting the site is renewing acquaintance with an old friend? These are some of the challenges this medium poses. How the designer responds we shall examine more fully later on, especially when discussing the relationship between the brand and the consumer (in 'Brand and consumer'). Meanwhile we need to return to the basics of the poster art.

People are not seduced into looking at posters by reading or viewing

A successful attempt to convey in one image a cinema idea – the change which the Smirnoff bottle imparts to a scene. Smirnoff, UK, 1996, Agency: Lowe Howard-Spink.

Not a word is changed of a well-known slogan, this time for a health club. The Edinburgh Club, UK, c1993, Agency: The Leith Agency.

something else. Contact is unplanned. Nevertheless, they have to be seduced in a very short time and generally from a distance. This is the challenge that drives the art, and puts simplicity at the top of the chart.

But, take note, simple does not mean simplistic, let alone simple-minded. Single-minded, yes. There are many examples (on these pages) of simple designs which communicate instantly, yet somehow stay in the mind. Attracting attention is important but involvement is critical, and, if possible, beginning a dialogue, a relationship.

The poster 'is to the eye what a shout is to the ear'.[14] Without the gaining of attention, subsequent dialogue is impossible. The eighteenth-century essayist Joseph Addison said, 'the great art of writing advertisements is the finding of the proper method to catch the reader's eye that without which a good thing may pass un-noticed.'[15]

The poster needs to stand out from its surroundings – to create 'an eye-arresting disturbance as different in texture from its environment as possible'. If not, or if the message is confused or the lettering unclear, the communication is frustrated. He who runs carries on running, none the wiser. Alain Weill, the French guru of the poster, says that of every three posters he is asked to judge at an annual festival he finds two hard to decipher. As if there is time! The creative director of a West Coast US agency never judges a poster at his desk: he asks the designer to hold it at head height and then runs past it!

72 *Another shout from a billboard.*
Perrier, France, 1995, Agency:
Publicis.

This, of course, is not the way to judge the idea, but the execution. We need to bear this in mind as we review the 'rules'.

1: Simplicity – nothing elaborate, ornate or complicated in the design or the verbal message.

2: One dominant image – though in expert hands this can be a collision or fusion of two images. Indeed many famous posters communicate two thoughts by means of a verbal and/or visual pun.

3: Boldness – the hoarding is no place for the half-gesture or subtle tone.

4: Clean, legible type – the poster is not a computer screen. Light or delicate lettering, closely spaced type or type superimposed upon a complicated background does not work at 50 metres.

5: Few words – six or seven – for immediate impact. If there are more (and there are interesting examples) the sentences need to be short.

6: Big enough type – i.e. large enough to be read from the specific distance for the particular site.

7: Contrasting colours – (preferably primary). Again, it is not the place for subtle nuances.

8: Brand (verb) – ensure not simply that the logo is big enough but that the whole design belongs to the brand (noun).

These are not new rules. However, it is reassuring to know that frequent and regular research reconfirms their truth. Outdoor contractor Maiden commissioned Research Services International to use its monthly poster

A simple, involving image thoroughly in character for Golf. (See also p 57). VW Golf, France, 1993 Agency: DDB.

WH Allner, Life Magazine, USA, c1950s.

Instant communication of a benefit. Symbolism means paring down to the essentials– a large pastille for a long throat. Niklaus Stoecklin, Gaba pastilles, Switzerland, 1937.

The revolutionary lettering says Polish but the advertiser makes sure in the caption. Zamoyski, UK, 1989, Agency: Davis Wilkins.

Brilliant and unforced use of the logo. Note, too, how the positioning of the camera case aids the composition. Herbert Leupin, Agfa, Switzerland, 1956.

Measure this design against the criteria above. G Hanspeter Rolly, Deiss shoes, Switzerland, 1983.

tracking study (RSL Signpost 1991–5) to identify 'certain creative factors that appeared to be related to poster effectiveness'. (Note the careful distinction between statistical and causal relationship.)

'Poor copy legibility tended to result in poor impact.' It needed no ghost to leave the grave to tell us this. Or that 'the use of colour helps to increase recognition and brand attribution and to enhance audience appeal'.[16]

In choosing colours there is a simple basic rule. High contrast rather than low. Blue and green is a low combination. Yellow out of red (or the reverse) is little better. Black out of yellow or white are at the high visibility end of the spectrum. Most advertising designers learn of the black/yellow combination in their formative years and some well-known brands and

posters have used these combinations to good effect. See the design for Ivens & Company, or the Zenit design by Marcello Dudovich. And the daddy of them all, Toulouse-Lautrec showed the way in the 'Divan Japonais'.

However, visibility isn't everything. Colours have meaning. A German company advertising in pre-war Czechoslovakia discovered that its dominant yellow and black posters resulted in decreasing sales because the Czechs hated those Habsburgian colours.

Branding, says the RSL Study, 'is vitally important for effective impact and in some cases appears to be more important than weight of spend'. However, when reviewing all the campaigns in their study they felt that 'only about one in five was well branded'. A sin of omission we shall return to.

74

Bernhard would probably have shown just the hat and the brand name. Dudovich does just that, dresses the set and hints at intrigue. Marcello Dudovich, Zenit, Borsalino, Italy, 1911.

Dudley Hardy manages to communicate the brand name and the assurance (and sex) of the users without really showing the product. Hardy, Phit-Eesi, UK, 1897.

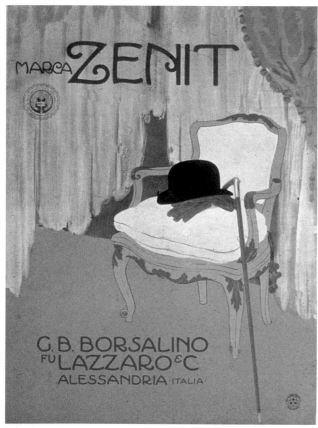

| BLACK | BLACK | YELLOW | WHITE | BLUE | WHITE | BLUE | YELLOW | GREEN |

It is a sin few of our early advertisers would understand, let alone commit. Registering the brand name was the prime purpose of the poster. As a brand develops priorities change but branding the offering remains, if not the purpose, then certainly a requirement.

Branding is not simply ensuring that the name is clear and dominant in the design but that the whole poster breathes its name. 'Is Brand Evident?' is the question I ask of any ad I judge. Is everything about the idea and the execution coherent and reflecting the brand personality? Those responsible for managing Guinness advertising in its heyday used to ask 'Is it Guinnessy?' The message and look had to be distinctively Guinness and there were rules to keep (see p 80). But over and above that was the spirit of the brand which permeated everything – advertising, design, behaviour.

Designer André François (who with Savignac was an assistant to Cassandre) believed that a poster 'should first of all be totally different in style, design and idea from its neighbours and competitors'.[17]

Please re-read that extract pausing on each of the five nouns. It was a Frenchman who said, 'Le style c'est l'homme lui meme'.[18] The style must express the brand. The design must be distinctive but true to the brand. The idea – the engine of the design – must be unique, distinguishable from not only direct competitors but also neighbouring advertisements. For all ads are competing for attention. And a familiar format or typeface or colour scheme can link disparate brands or services. A hardware retailer

Just a soupçon of Art Nouveau, but controlled – and the lady is as composed as the design. The work of Holland's first true poster artist. JG van Caspel, Ivens, The Netherlands, 1900.

Henri de Toulouse-Lautrec, Divan Japonais, France, 1893.

WHITE BROWN WHITE BROWN YELLOW RED WHITE RED YELLOW

which chose to abandon its corporate colour for a seasonal green at Christmas was mistaken for a fashion chain.

The poster needs to stand out. 'Just imagine', says François, 'the effect of a Fragonard in an exhibition of abstract painting – or vice versa'. Today, standing out is less difficult to achieve since outdoor ads are less cheek by jowl. Nevertheless, there is the context to think of, the environment in which the poster is viewed. If the *brand is evident*[19] then the ad has registered its true identity. Now if much of this seems obvious, why do so many executions ignore the precepts? The facile answer is that nobody creates with rules. Certainly not. Nor does the artist create with the frame. Nevertheless, the discipline of the frame serves a creative purpose.

Less glib is the rejoinder that if all designers followed the same precepts all designs would be, if not identical, monotonously similar. Undoubtedly a city of yellow and black posters would prove tiresome. But this misses the point. Besides, the guidelines recommend contrast: they do not specify which.

Moreover, the colours have first to be appropriate to the brand and the message. Do they call for colours that come at the viewer, advancing colours such as yellow, orange and red which convey heat, excitement, fire, sun? Or are receding colours more suitable – green, blue, violet with their evocation of coolness and serenity, of sky and distance and water?

Study examples in this book. Ask yourself whether the choice of colours is arbitrary. Would it matter if other colours were substituted? What effect

76 *Herbert Leupin, Swiss Railway, Switzerland, 1958.*

Another example of Leupin's visual punning. Herbert Leupin, Suze, Switzerland, 1955.

would it have? Take, for example, four designs by the Swiss artist Herbert Leupin. How would his Swiss Railway design look with a lighter background? Would the Suze lettering be as striking, or the Coca-Cola message (see p 78) as compelling without the yellow or the red? Finally, the *Tribune* newspaper (see p 78) – why the red? The last example reminds us that the product category itself makes certain demands. Newspapers, despite recent technology, are black and white. Mineral waters are tinged with blue; countries have the colour schemes of their flags; wines are red, white or rosé, and beer shades of brown; milk is white and so on.

Similarly a brand's own name may constrain the brand colours – Orangina, Yellow Pages, Red Stripe, Black Label, Blue Band. Alternatively,

Brand colours

Red	Coca-Cola, Marlboro, KitKat
Blue	Nivea, Contrex
Green	Benetton, Perrier
Yellow	Kodak
Purple	Silk Cut, Cadbury's
Green/Yellow	BP
Yellow/Blue	Ikea
Blue/Black	BMW
Red/Black	Nike
Red/Yellow	Shell
Black	Guinness

When tobacco companies were prevented from promising anything, Benson & Hedges became abstract. The Government copy only adds to the surreality. UK, 1978, Agency: CDP.

Draught Guinness takes a little while to settle. Guinness, Ireland, 1996, Agency: HHCL.

The KitKat red dominates the London taxi, UK, 1995, Agency: J Walter Thompson.

MIDDLE TAR As defined by H.M.Government
EVERY PACKET CARRIES A GOVERNMENT HEALTH WARNING

if one brand of a product has appropriated a colour or combination of colours another brand which adopts the same may end up helping the competition.

The good designer knows about constraints, has presumably studied laws of form, colour, composition, contrast, proportion, dynamics and so on. Constraints go with the territory. He or she does not succumb to them but works with them. The precepts, like any set of guidelines, are meant to help, tools rather than rules. They are the result of practical experience. If the designer chooses to ignore them, so be it – a conscious decision rather than an ignorant act.

The tools are designed to help the advertiser deliver a short, compelling – and hopefully involving – message whilst competing for attention with the distractions of life in the open air. For, if one of outdoor's strengths is the fact of outdoors – where people live and work and play and congregate and travel – the pursuit of these activities is their primary purpose, not the perusing of posters. Paul Rand speaks of the need to create visual ideas appropriate to the medium:

> Countless so-called posters are not posters at all – they are merely enlarged illustrations which ignore the fundamental, functional consideration of size, distant viewing, and speed of the viewer which should be the determinants of poster design.[20]

Getting an idea across in this environment is difficult. Just how difficult has rarely been better described than by Doug Linton of ACLC, Canada:

An essential part of the morning ritual. Herbert Leupin, Tribune newspaper, Switzerland, 1955.

The fewer the words the more you convey, particularly if, as here, the words 'work' in more than one language. Herbert Leupin, Coca-Cola, Switzerland, 1953.

Creating exciting, memorable Outdoor is as close as you can get to working without a net. You're not fighting for space on a page, there's no room for support copy to flush out a blind headline. You haven't got 30 or 45 or 60 seconds to make sure you get your point across. Outdoor is the unadorned quest for attention and retention, the ultimate distillation of a message. To succeed in Outdoor is to pass the supreme creative test.[21]

The early masters of poster invariably passed the test. Chéret attracted attention by means of a dynamic woman at the centre of the design. So did Fred Walker in what could be called the first British poster, 'The Woman in White'. Text is integrated in the image. Key information is instantly grasped. Less important elements are less immediate.

In the UK Dudley Hardy and, particularly, the Beggarstaffs – and later, Bernhard in Germany – reduced the elements and restricted their use of colour – sacrifices at the altar of impact. The figures are not unlike silhouettes and are clearly as dramatic. M. de Silhouette was a French minister of finance in the 1750s. He insisted on economy in all things with the result that the public used his name to describe anything cheap. Economy in design is powerful. Less is more.

Surely the designer needs all the help he can get – even if the tools are old. And executional tools do not determine the idea, they help the designer express it. They are the means by which the designer can confront the limitations he has been set. Not so much fighting them but exploiting them.

Outside Vaison la Romaine in Provence, a sign on an old door indicates a junk sale on France's national day in a nearby village, 1996.

Poster rules, 1938

A variant on 'good for you' and much
more involving. Gilroy, Guinness, UK,
1936, Agency: SH Benson.

'Life was easier then', you'll hear admen say. But sixty years ago – as these extracts show – constraints were *de rigueur*.

The Guinness rules and Eno's criteria, opposite, have lessons today.

They were published in the trade quarterly, the *Poster,* respectively in April and October 1938.

The Ingredients
(a) All humorous Guinness posters have been exclusively designed by the same artist (Gilroy).
(b) All Guinness posters use the slogan, 'Guinness is good for you', or variations deriving from it ('Guinness for strength', 'My Goodness – My Guinness', etc.) over and over again.
(c) All Guinness posters use a very readable blockletter-type for the slogans.
(d) All slogans on Guinness posters appear uniform in red.
(e) All Guinness posters show plenty of white space, which makes them stand out on hoardings from their competitors.
(f) All Guinness posters are surrounded by a black-and-green border.
(g) All Guinness posters show the same technique for illustrating the product.

Guinness used approximately 32,000 posters, of which 2,000 were 64 sheet (3 metres by 8). 'Strength' was the theme – but treated humorously in a time of depression. The switch to 'My Goodness' occurred in 1935.

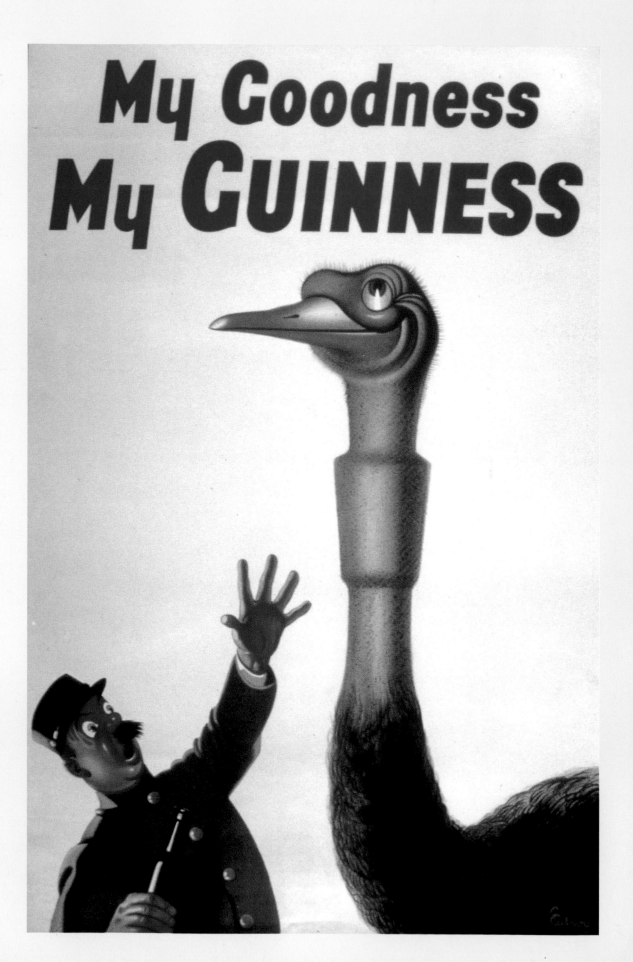

A hallmark of the brand's advertising was topicality. Here the artist Gilroy ties in with the demolition of a London landmark. Guinness, UK, 1934, Agency: SH Benson.

Another Gilroy, Guinness, UK, 1935, Agency: SH Benson.

'Guinness is good for you' was the brand's slogan for decades. In the 1970s advertising's self-regulatory body queried the claim. However, reversing the message could not be questioned. Guinness, UK, 1988, Agency: Allen, Brady and Marsh.

WATERLOO BRIDGE is coming down

GUINNESS FOR STRENGTH

GUINNESS

FOR STRENGTH

Ask These Ten Questions About Your Humorous Poster

1. Is the poster guying the product? Is the product ridiculed, or is the laugh with the product?
2. Is the product's name part of the joke? (Otherwise the public will remember the joke, but not the product.)
3. Are the chief selling points incorporated in the joke?
4. Does the cartoonist not overshadow the product? (Some cartoonists have such a definite style of their own that you can tell immediately the designer, but not the product.)
5. Is the joke in a popular vein … or 'highbrow'? (If it makes directors laugh that is no evidence that it will make the people in the street laugh. Show your poster to typical members of the public and see what their reaction is.)
6. Is the joke within the limits of good taste? Does it ridicule the public (your customers!) or institutions to the point of offence?
7. Do cartoon and copy 'overlap'? Does the copy explain what the cartoon already shows?
8. Will the joke withstand the effects of repetition? (Are amusing details incorporated in the cartoon which the public will only notice after seeing the poster several times?)
9. Does the joke lend itself to an extension into a series of humorous posters? (And possibly into a follow-up series.)
10. Is the joke so amusing that you would tell it to your friends? Does it incite (gratis) word-of-mouth publicity?

GUINNLESS isn't good for you

The creative person or team has to get it right in the shortest possible expression, unaided by context. This provides a creative discipline as strict as the verse form for the poet.

But, as we know, rules can be broken. And situations in which the poster is seen vary. A shout may be valid on the highway but on a railway platform or in an airport lounge there is time for something more – maybe with fewer decibels – conversation even, in the carriage. Indeed, in a taxicab there may actually be sufficient time for a heart-to-heart (see p185).

Outdoor is a varied medium and each variety has its own specific strengths and applications. To use outdoor merely to show a commercial's end shot 'writ large' is to miss a trick, but to regard a car card as a billboard 'writ small' is equally perverse. Though there are occasions (and reasons) which justify ignoring the rules, it must be remembered that they were engendered by the discipline of the medium. The professional poster artist understands this. Few have defined the task as cogently as Manfred Reiss:

> Now to my mind a good poster is one which is not overcrowded, never conveys more than one idea at a time, stands out from its surroundings, is bold and colourful, has the minimum of words and the symbol it introduces (drawn, photographic, or a combination of both) is quickly and easily understood.[22]

The discipline which engendered the rules also provided a potent creative stimulus – and that is the subject of the next chapter.

82 *Coca-Cola posters are rarely complicated. Simple, almost naïve at times, but always strongly branded. Coca-Cola, USA, 1945.*

*An original way to demonstrate
the strength of the brand. Levi
Strauss, Italy, 1992,
Agency: McCann-Erickson.*

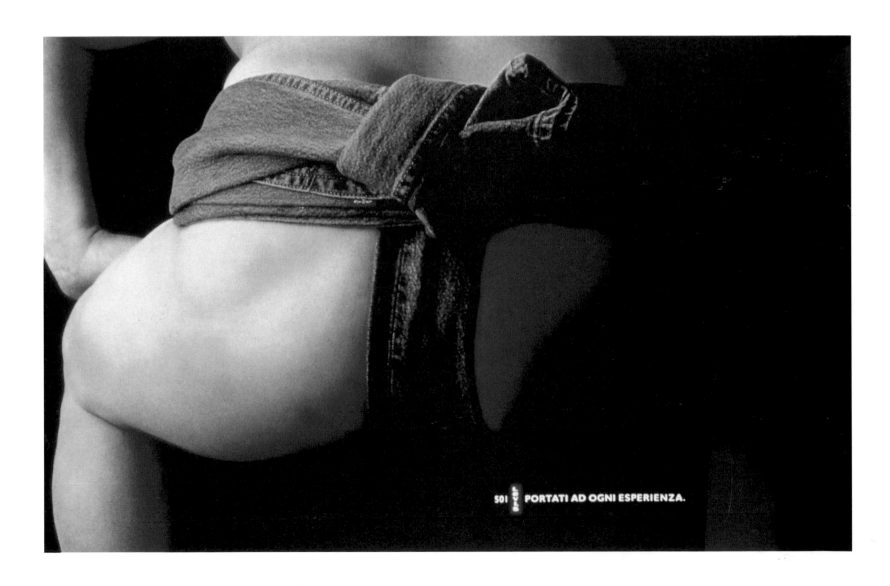

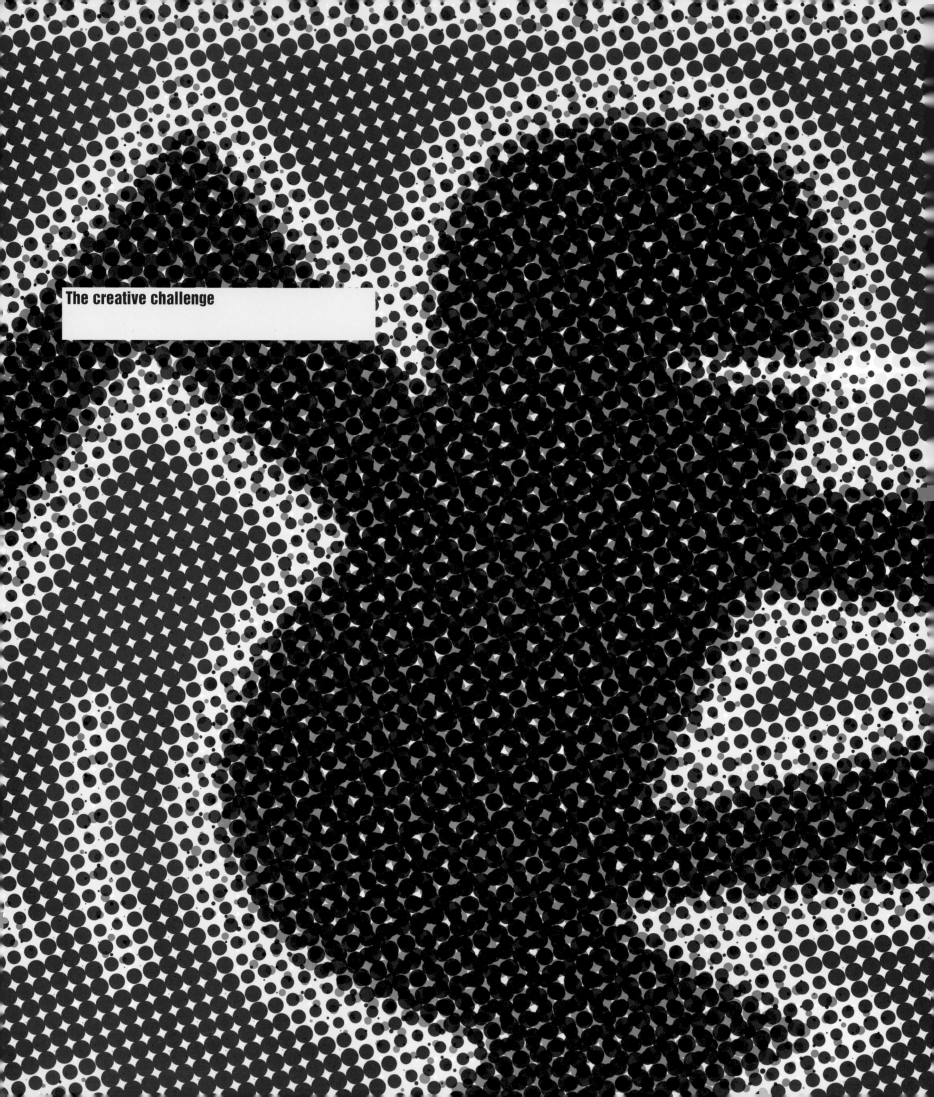

The creative challenge

'Set an architect free in a large field and command him there to design a building and he will produce something ordinary. Place him in a confined environment and he will excel himself.' So observes product designer and Pentagram partner, Kenneth Grange.[1]

A primary school teacher sets the class a weekly essay. One day she says, 'Today children you can write about anything you like.' There is much chewing of pens and scratching of heads. But when she says, 'Today the subject is *castles*', pens flow and minds create.

The great posters are triumphs of imagination set free by limitation. They succeed not despite, but because of, the constraints. Discipline is the midwife of ideas. Savignac defined the idea as the spice of a poster.

'Whereas the form affects only the retina, the idea penetrates the mind and the heart. It is the egg of Columbus – the solution which seems so exceedingly simple *after* it has been thought of.'[2]

Surprisingly simple. My job as creative director was to be surprised. I had to create an environment in which ideas could happen, ideas which would surprise me. I stole the thought from Sergei Diaghilev. The impresario used to greet the brilliant, young Jean Cocteau each morning with the words 'Jean, étonne moi'.

Good ads surprise though not all surprising ads are good. Surprise is of two sorts. The first is a reaction of astonishment or wonder at a new thought or connection. The second is a flash of realization, the blinding glimpse of

86 *Good ideas are often obvious – afterwards. Triumph cars, UK, 1981, Agency: Saatchi and Saatchi.*

Raymond Savignac was in demand not only in his native France but in the UK, USA and most of Western Europe. Savignac, Il Giorno newspaper, Italy, 1956.

the obvious. Obvious, that is, only after it has been pointed out. Seeing something familiar, something you have seen a hundred times for the very first time. The reaction to the first type of surprise is 'wow!'. To the second – 'of course!' – accompanied by a slap of hand on head or a pained smile and the words 'Why didn't I think of that?' … which generally means – since the idea was there the whole time, floating about in the ether – 'Why didn't that think of me?'

A poster for the Triumph TR7 open-top sports car says, 'Now with a little extra headroom – 93 million miles'. Why did it take a hundred years from the invention of the car for anyone (in this case, a Saatchi creative team) to see it, to make the connection? Ideas happen when two thoughts come into collision. A window becomes a newspaper (*Il Giorno*). A thermos is a 'Hip Flask'. A poster for a church is a sign from God. Emu knitting wool plus a pair of needles become an emu.

'If a poster is any good you have to look twice to see what's going on', says Otto Treumann. 'You're intrigued … what have I actually seen? … look at it again. Only then do you really discover it.'[3] The second look may be a split second later – or the next time you pass the site.

Artists and ad persons make the strange familiar or, more frequently, the familiar strange. In launch advertising, the former, something new is made accessible. In maintenance advertising of an existing brand, a case of the latter, something taken for granted suddenly isn't: the brand is refreshed.

Emu seems a strange name for a wool – until the artist knits a connection. FHK Henrion, Emu wool, UK, 1958.

A redesigned product – a new view of the brand. Thermos, UK, 1995, Agency: TBWA.

The devil doesn't have all the best jokes. St Phillip the Deacon, Lutheran Church, USA, 1995, Agency: HMS/Ruhr.

Guinness, Oxo, Persil … all are brands of pensionable age. All have been continually refreshed. It is no coincidence that one agency, J Walter Thompson, has been connected with all three. Its ex-chairman Jeremy Bullmore refuses to believe in the occasionally fashionable theory of brand cycle – namely that brands, like people, are born, mature and inevitably die. This is a cop out, he says (though more eloquently) – which means it's not the company's fault, or the agency's, but God's.[4]

A brand which continues to surprise will never die. But surprise has to be relevant. Right as well as bright. It is easy to surprise irrelevantly. Bill Bernbach famously observed that you can show a man upside-down but unless you are promoting a pair of trousers with pockets from which coins

do not drop out you are merely attracting interest only to frustrate it.

A Danish poster for Ramlösa mineral water shows the bottle upside-down – plus the line 'One for the road'. But then upside-down is how bottles appear on the wall behind a bar. Savignac similarly is justified in showing one man upside-down in his Astral paint design conveying in one image the two markets for paint, the professional and the handyman. But there is less reason for Procter & Gamble (of all people!) putting half of the image in their Belgian Dash billboard the wrong way up, unless, as has been suggested, the board was positioned alternately – first one way, then the other.

Irrelevant surprise is common: jokes for their own sake, self-indulgent conceits, unrelated images. The result of irrelevant surprise is rejection: the

88 *A relevant surprise. Ramlösa,*
Denmark, 1994, Agency: Ted Bates.

Raymond Savignac conveys that both professional and handyman do better with the brand. Note how the thought is reinforced, and given a second meaning, by the vertical messages. Savignac, Astral, France, 1949.

viewer feels conned. The result of relevant surprise is revelation: it reveals something about the brand or one's relationship with it or, even, something about oneself.

The masters of the art knew all about the need to surprise. Perhaps shock would be a better word. 'The poster must penetrate,' said Cassandre, 'not like a gentleman going through the door with a painting on an easel, but like a burglar through the window with a crowbar in his hand.'[5]

'A good poster', said Savignac, 'shatters the wall just as a great actor shatters the screen. Any means of achieving this goal is justified: lyricism, caprice, eroticism, tears, mystification, bribery, cynicism … anything but modesty.'[6]

There is an apocryphal story of an Irishman in a focus group who, on being asked his opinion of a brand, replied, 'the adver*tise*ments speak highly of it.' I wish sometimes that brands would brag a little more. The trouble with reticence is that one begins to suspect that lights are being hidden under bushels due to low wattage.

'Anything but modesty.' What can be added under 'anything'? Energy, enthusiasm (if the advertiser isn't enthusiastic about the brand who will be?).

Cappiello would probably add a third E, 'exaggeration', to Savignac's list – a pack enlarged, a feature emphasized, an element grotesquely out of proportion. But it would always be one element – a single factor to pierce the consciousness of the passer-by and to stay in the memory.

Unorthodox media buying perhaps but the message hits home to the passengers as they survey passing luggage and anticipate collecting the car. Volvo, airports, 1990s.

A colours message one way up: a whites message the other. The board, presumably, was displayed alternately on different sites. Dash, Belgium, 1992, Agency: Leo Burnett.

The poster is a paradox. It offers the advertising creative team the widest canvas and the narrowest discipline, tougher than any other medium. As we have already noted, the poster's chief discipline is not space (what could be bigger than the side of a bus?) but time.

Time, however, is not constant. It stretches when you want it to hurry, accelerates when you wish it to stop. The time spent on an outdoor ad by the passer-by may depend on his or her mood, ignorance or knowledge, interest in the category, identification with the brand, a traffic jam, or whether he or she is waiting for a bus or a lover.

But the constraints of time, together with speed and distance, make the artist's canvas in a sense much smaller. Erik Bruun, the Finnish designer, recommends that the poster should be designed in a space no larger than a matchbox cover. [7]

The brief forces the team, the designer, to concentrate initially on the idea rather than the execution. Our bastard artist, working in the middle of the inexact science, is fed a brief. This discipline is a business necessity: it ensures that the solution fits the agreed purpose of the communication. It is also a creative necessity: it acts as a stimulus. The brief provides a focus for the creative team.

Communication begins at the end. End has two meanings – finish and purpose. All communicators – in print, on television, on a platform or a hoarding – must start by putting themselves in the receiver's position, by

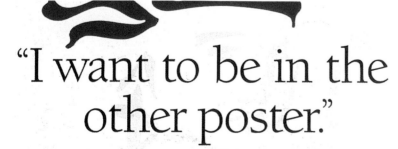

thinking like the listener, viewer or passer-by. Clearly they must also understand the objective, the purpose of the communication.

All the preliminary 'science' of research and planning and analysis should result in a brief of a single page. Each agency has its own language and sub-headings, but at the heart is the proposition. What benefit are we offering the consumer? Buttressing this will be 'reason-why' (justification for purchase) and a 'target response', a sentence expressed colloquially, i.e. not in adspeak but in the consumer's language, conveying the reaction the communication is intended to provoke.

Here are a few imagined target responses deduced from outdoor ads featured on these pages. They should not prove too difficult to identify.

(Alternatively examine ads on the street and ask yourself what each advertiser intends the consumer to think, believe, feel and/or do as a result. You may find this difficult. Don't worry it's not your fault.)

'If it's good enough for the Queen it's good enough for me.'

'They really mean big discounts. It would be silly not to go there first.'

'I'll remember that next time I fill up.'

'It is the best ... I suppose I *can* afford it.'

But the key is the proposition – and the shorter and sharper the better. A paragraph, better still a sentence. One creative director, Dave Trott, asks for 'one word and a thousand facts'. He is happy to delve among supporting factual material provided he has focus, direction, 'one word'.[8]

Bright use of complementary sites on a bus shelter. Sky TV, UK, 1996, Agency: The Clinic.

Cows and effect

Every body needs milk. Milk Advisory Board, USA, 1980.

Mejerierna, Sweden, 1985, Agency: Hall & Cederquist.

Martin Steinemann, Dairy Central Propaganda, Switzerland, 1970.

Joseph Binder, Austria, 1928.

We all know what milk looks like so it's hardly necessary to show the product. Only one of these designs pictures it. Two disregard illustration altogether. The Swiss, appealing to patriotism, and the Brits, in commending an abstract, don't actually promise much. Cows are promised happiness. One is certainly energetic, as is the only human depicted. And the walrus makes an incisive point about calcium.

MILCH. MUNTERMACHER DER NATUR.

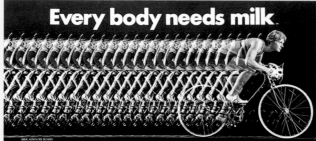

Every body needs milk

PUBLICITÉ   PL. 1

Milch

AUF JEDEM TISCH

Dina tänder behöver kalcium.
MJÖLK

Milk Producers Association, Bern, Switzerland, 1994, Agency: Advico Young & Rubicam.

Milk Marketing Association, UK, 1970s Agency: Mather & Crowther (subsequently Ogilvy & Mather).

Michigan Milk Producers Association, USA, 1980s.

93

The creative task is difficult but it is very simple to define. It is to turn a proposition into an idea. An idea is a proposition ignited by imagination. A proposition may occasionally be enough by itself. If the brand represents a breakthrough, offers a unique benefit, then simply stating the rational attribute may suffice. However, competition may catch up and offer the identical benefit. What will differentiate brand A from brand B? Not the what but the how, the way that attribute has been expressed. The creative task is therefore not simply shaping the proposition but transmuting it. It should turn the prose of the proposition into the poetry of the idea. Poetry makes meaning more meaningful. The idea must resonate with the intended consumer.

Einstein, in the most compressed metaphor of physics, described matter as frozen energy. A proposition is a frozen idea. Imagination does the defrosting. For within the proposition are leads to constituents which will come together, collide, to make the idea.

The proposition for a chewing gum is something like this: unlike other chewing gums, Trident has a taste that lasts. The idea is the line integrated with the appropriate and obvious graphic: 'Stretch the taste'.

Integration (fusion) is key. The proposition for Bally is that they make stylish shoes for both men and women. Simple but dual. In the hands of a lesser designer it could lack focus. Renato Hauser solves the design problem by means of a shadow – and no words other than the brand name.

94

A neat fusion of two thoughts. The visual treatment avoids any unpleasantness. Trident, Switzerland, 1995.

'Bally make classic shoes for men and sophisticated shoes for women' could have been the brief. Renato Hauser, Bally, Switzerland, 1986, Agency: Doyle Dane Bernbach.

Compare the US billboards for Gas and the Falcon car. The proposition for the first is that smart women cook by gas. Which of course is exactly the message of the ad: the proposition is the idea (if that's the word). No transmutation has taken place. All that has been added to the proposition is dressing. With Falcon the proposition is quite simply that here is a car that will satisfy both the male and female driver. The idea of the two gloved hands competing for the key not only communicates the basic proposition but suggests the macho and style elements of the car though showing you nothing of it. Branding, however, is strong. Compare also the static quality of the gas poster with the tension and movement of the Falcon ad.

The Buick Riviera board is not an idea but merely a statement of the proposition: 'adventure'. The same criticism can be levelled at the New Haven Railroad poster (see p 119). If the picture says it there is no need for the words. If the picture doesn't then it's back to the drawing board.

The Micra is a much smaller car. It has a distinctive shape, simple and driver-friendly. Much of this was conveyed on posters by means of the outline drawing (what could be simpler?) and a line of copy. Supplementary text appeared in print. Then came a brief to stress fuel economy. The idea was to equate the small size of the Micra with the microdot of petrol emerging from the nozzle of the fuel pump. A strong graphic hyperbole which is nevertheless true to the spirit of the brief.

The brief (with the proposition at the heart) serves three purposes. It sets

A proposition merely re-stated.
Gas, USA, 1950–72.

If you have to say it, it may mean you haven't shown it. Buick, USA, 1963–4, Agency: McCann-Erickson.

A proposition imaginatively transmuted. Falcon cars, USA, 1962.

the problem and at the end provides the criteria by which it may be judged. And in between it acts as a creative tool. It is a mental gymnasium.

Now, as if the constraints of the brief aren't enough, the poster adds its own – limited time, minimal support, distance, a moving audience.

Musicologists assess a composer's worth by his or her chamber works. A string quartet is the pure musical idea unassisted by orchestration. The poster is advertising's string quartet. The idea is all. (Or at least it should be.) And it is far easier to assess the creativity of a poster than advertisements in other media. Advertisers, on being shown a campaign in several media, though not outdoor, are apt to command, 'Show me the Poster'.[9] Similarly, an agency's creative director will ask creative teams to

prepare a poster even if outdoor is not contemplated in the media schedule. The poster is the focus medium. If it works as a poster it will work elsewhere. The reverse is nowhere near as universal a truth.

A poster reduced for a magazine will communicate. A magazine ad enlarged on a hoarding will rarely do so. However, to the reader who scans the page – or the passenger seated opposite a newspaper reader – a press ad needs to act as a poster.

A recent and successful press campaign for Boddington's beer has appeared exclusively on the coloured back pages of magazines. They are, to all intents and purposes, posters.

The medium forces the designer to concentrate on the essence of the

How a car ad gets noticed: the comic interpretation of the new Micra. Nissan Micra, UK, 1992, Agency: TBWA.

A neatly located follow-up for the economical car. Nissan Micra, UK, 1993, Agency: TBWA.

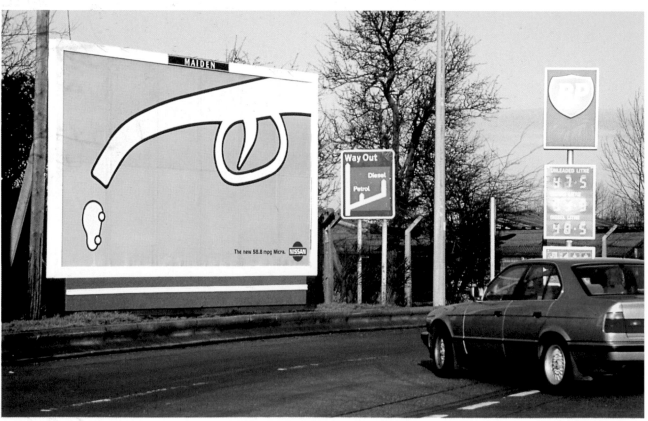

brand promise. If the brief is one word then the design, though maybe fusing two thoughts, is one element. Look at the work of Leonetto Cappiello, Villemot, Games, Cassandre, Savignac, Henrion – it is the art of reduction. Kyösti Varis calls posters 'extremely reduced visual renditions'.[10] 'It puts your ideas on a diet', says a current promotional piece from the OAAA.

The German-born US painter Hans Hoffman says, 'The ability to simplify means to eliminate the unnecessary so that the necessary may speak.'[11]

'The leaving out of detail is as important as the underlining of essentials', said RA Stephens in 1924.[12] 'Throwing out is more important than bringing in', echoed Abram Games, three decades later.[13]

Voltaire defined poetry's essence as concentration. It 'says more and in fewer words than prose.'[14] The graphic image says more with less than the proposition. Alain Weill compares good design with the Japanese haiku, the seventeen-syllable poem, 'the extreme synthesis of thought that is the essence of a good poster'.[15]

The verbal or visual pun, where two thoughts or images are fused, works harder than the two constituents separately. It is the difference between metaphor and simile. Where simile says, look this thing is like that thing, metaphor says this thing *is* that thing. 'My love is like a red, red rose' is simile.[16] 'The yellow fog that rubs its back against the window panes' is metaphor. A metaphor is a simile with its sleeves rolled up. (And that's a metaphor.)

The beer is the cream of Manchester.
Boddington's, Whitbread, UK,
1992–6, Agency: Bartle Bogle
Hegarty.

The ad in the press works as a
poster.

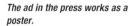

'It's The Real Thing'…

… said Coca-Cola. But real what? –
refreshment, enjoyment, fun,
whatever you wish presumably.
But in the case of a product
containing real *fruit* how can
the fact be communicated?

 'Peel A Can Today' said a Del
Monte poster in the Sixties. Here
are other attempts to reassure
consumers, to fuse brand name
and authentic content.

TriNaranjus, Mexico, 1993.

Zuko, Chile, 1994.

Bernard Villemot, Orangina,
France, 1965.

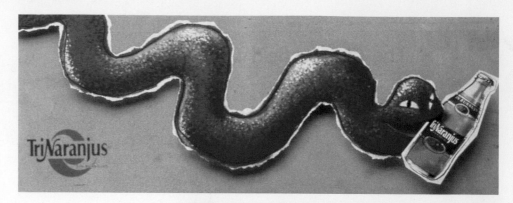

Life Savers, Canada, 1980s, Agency:
Young & Rubicam.

Tropic, Finland, 1996,
Agency: SEK & Grey.

The image is a fusion. So is the
headline (akta = real). 'Full of sun
ripened tomatoes', says the text,
maybe unnecessarily.
Felix sauce, Sweden, 1984,
Agency: Intermarco Farmer.

'Bovril prevents that sinking feeling' – with the pyjama-clad man aboard the jar afloat on the ocean – is so familiar that the brilliance of the craft (of poster artist HH Harris) may be lost. In one graphic image and slogan he conveys the promise of the brand whilst making sure that the brand is the hero. The cliché of sinking (i.e. lack of energy due to hunger) is given surprising impact. The word is seen anew via the image. Then in 'Bovril puts beef into you' note how the verbal pun ('beef') is illustrated in a graphic which, by hyperbole, represents the benefit of consuming the brand.

Compressing – as Bovril does – before and after into one image is a perpetual challenge. Coppertone achieves it via the dog tearing away the child's swimming trunks, revealing the brand's benefit. Derma Plast shows

the progression from tears to smile – and the reason – in one engaging image (see p107). The Swedish tonic Samarin uses a mask (before) revealing a real face (after). Vittel uses the same device thirty years later. Note here too the visual pun of the victory sign and the capital V.

Side by side to show before and after is logical but less impactful. It is more suited to other media. For example Heineken's long-running television campaign is a narrative humorously illustrating the brand's ability to refresh parts 'other beers cannot reach' and thus relieve or ameliorate a distressful or awkward situation. The creative team, in transferring to outdoor, chose to treat the medium as a storyboard or comic strip, rather than revisiting the idea and finding a graphic expression. Subsequently, though, in a press ad,

Before and after. Bovril, UK, 1925, Agency: SH Benson.

A long-running Bovril poster. HH Harris, UK, 1925, Agency: SH Benson.

Before and after. Frank Craig, Coppertone, USA, campaign began 1953.

Vittel, France, 1978, Agency: CLM/BBDO.

After over-indulgence take Samarin and smile. Note the part played by the mask is the reverse of Vittel. Töre Hinnerud, Samarin, Sweden, 1950.

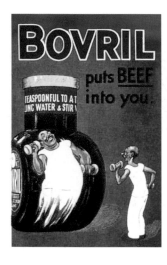

they used a subsidiary line from the commercial – 'Only Heineken can do this' – which worked far better, using a single end-result visual.

Kraft, wishing to feature the real fruit origin of their jam, shows the progression of berry to conserve in a series of five pictures. The message is better conveyed on a poster by instant transition in a single image.

'Brevity is the soul of wit' (Shakespeare)[17] and lingerie (Dorothy Parker).[18] Note brief and brevity have the same roots. 'Art is limitation. The essence of every picture', said GK Chesterton, 'is the frame.'

Hans Schleger (Zero) reduced the concept of creative discipline to three words: 'limitation produces form'.[19] Deny the poster artist movement then he has to convey it. Deny him time and he has to expand it. Deny him words

then the words he chooses not merely have to work harder, they have to grow. Provide a peculiar or restricted format and he will exploit it.

Another challenge is movement. It can be depicted in crude speed lines or more subtly via gradations. Op Art arguably appeared first on the hoardings. Cassandre in 1935 used circles for Nicolas. Severo Pozzati (or Sepo as he reduced it) conveyed the speed of the DKW motorcycle by bending the brand's initials, quadrupling the image and shooting out the bike as if an arrow from a strung bow. Sepo it was who sliced the Motta cake and used perspective to show the slices tumbling. Dudovich made *Il Giornale d'Italia* come alive with a dance of the eight sheets. Josep Morrell captures movement for Molfort's silk socks by excessive gesture.

The 'essentially television' campaign idea is almost literally translated into a storyboard. Heineken, UK, 1975, Agency: Collett Dickenson Pearce & Partners.

Another sequence. For more imaginative transformations of fruit into product see the spread on the previous pages. Kraft, Canada, 1989, Agency: J Walter Thompson.

That sinking feeling from Hungary. The product is a bitter herbal digestive. Emperor Franz Josef, it is told, upon trying the drink said it was unique. Hence the brand name. Unicum, Hungary, 1920s.

Using the end line of the commercial allows the story to be told in one image – with the participation of the reader. Press ad. Heineken, UK, 1991, Agency: Lowe Howard-Spink.

Heineken. Refreshes the parts other beers cannot reach.

Only Heineken can do this.

For the Purist.

Shell classically achieved it with a two-headed man and the line 'That's Shell that was'. It is not generally realized that neither the image nor the line was the original idea. Indeed ideas are rarely born fully formed and beautiful, arising like Venus from a shell as in Botticelli's painting. In my experience it involves effort, mess and forceps delivery. It also takes a trained eye and imagination to recognize the potential. The original line was 'That's Shell that is', spoken by an observer of a speeding car. A member of the public wrote to Shell suggesting the double headed visual and the altered slogan. The proposition: 'Shell makes your car go fast'. The idea: 'That's Shell that was!' The idea communicates the same message but heightens it. Meaning is made more meaningful.

Today movement can be real (see 'Beyond the billboard'). Or a spectacular which breaks the bounds of the site can dramatically convey movement. An actual Volkswagen emerges from the supersite which bears the headline, 'The only way to fly'. But is it any more mobile than the lithograph by Paul Colin which uses a repeated tree impression and an angled car to depict the 1935 Peugeot's acceleration? Or compare the movement in the brilliant Belgian Nike poster. Three elements across the middle of the narrow board: racquet, Agassi (head and shoulders) and ball. Agassi's hand holds the racquet and his eyes hold the ball. This is movement caught but not annihilated.

Movement and/or the passage of time can be imaginatively conveyed in outdoor by the use of two sites, side by side – as in the simple pairing

102

Severo Pozzati (Sepo), DKW, Italy, 1934.

Severo Pozzati, Motta, Italy, 1933.

Josep Morrell, Molfort's silk socks, Spain, 1929.

John Reynolds, Shell, UK, 1930.

Marcello Dudovich, Il Giornale d'Italia, Italy, c1902.

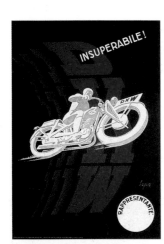

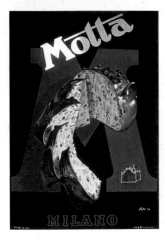

by Leupin for Bata shoes – or better still with a gap between them to show, for example, a biscuit jumping out of a pack, or a young girl blowing out the candles on her birthday cake or a basketball player throwing a ball from one site into the basket on the other.

Similarly, actual passage of time can be utilized by posting the same site twice. The Volkswagen Memphis question and answer posted over two months is an example of this. As is the Swedish Nokia teaser campaign (see p 172). In Switzerland Kodak Gold II was preceded on the hoarding by a curtained teaser. In Japan Lacoste was launched – or rather hatched – by means of a series of six posters. In 1992 Friends of the Earth demonstrated the presence and effect of acid rain in London by posting large pieces of litmus paper and inviting passers-by to watch them change colour.

Distance between sites can also be utilized. An early example is the US Burma Shave campaign of doggerel messages divided into six individual one foot by three foot boards set 100 feet apart along the highway. For example: Does your husband/misbehave/grunt and groan/rant and rave/shoot the brute/some Burma Shave. In Finland Fuji film, with strategically positioned lamp-post signs, informs the passing motorist or passenger that three reels can be purchased for the price of two.

One of outdoor's traditional weak points was topicality. Today technology enables the site contractor to change the message frequently (see 'Beyond the billboard'). But in the past one had to rely on ingenuity and hardwork.

Paul Colin conveys speed by angle, speedlines and shadows. Colin, Peugeot, France, 1935.

What's in the box – and would you buy it? Days later the first question is answered. VW Golf Memphis, France, 1997, Agency: DDB Needham.

A cheap and effective device for adjacent bills. Herbert Leupin, Bata shoes, Switzerland, 1954.

Cropping, composition, consummate craft. Who needs technology? Nike, Belgium, 1995, Agency: Quattro DMB.

In San Francisco, a financial services company E A Pierce employed a team of painters to inscribe the Dow Jones index every hour. The Waterman's pen company was able to paint a map of Europe plus a fountain pen and erect it within hours of the signing of the armistice in 1918. In 1938 Ovaltine stuck labels to its posters to announce a radio campaign. In World War Two the *Los Angeles Times* won a top national award for the best media promotion. The billboard featured a different headline every day. In Trafalgar Square each midnight for a month in 1966 when The Times removed advertising from its front page and relaunched itself, a team of agency people put up the next day's headlines two at a time (hanging up individual letters) on a rotating trivision site. Huge poster sites for retailers could still feature the day's special offer by devoting a small section to a paste-on paper sheet or 'snipe'. In the last decade the *Minneapolis St Paul Star Tribune* daily newspaper had a new board painted every morning.

Some structures allow part of the sign to move. Badoit used the moving part to carry a continuous message. Dunlop used tri-vision to illustrate three different products. The UK Electricity Council used the sequence to demonstrate how quickly a halogen hob heats up. In Bombay a board for a mobile phone features a changing electronic digital display. In the same city more traditional art is currently employed for Amul butter. Each week there appears a painted cartoon on a topical subject, related, however tenuously, to the brand.

104

Successive pillar signs inform the driver that three Fuji films can be had for the price of two. Fuji, Finland, 1995.

Hourly Dow Jones changes painted on a board. EA Pierce, USA, 1934.

Erected within hours of signing of the Armistice. Waterman pens, USA, 1918.

The medium's limitations – time, movement, topicality, restricted information – are less intimidating today thanks to technology and the breaking of constraints. Outdoor is no longer strictly two-dimensional. A real car can not only jump out of a sign, but, in the case of Araldite in the UK, be stuck to it to demonstrate adhesion. A decade later another car appeared stuck, this time to a Dutch billboard. Beneath it was a picture of a pack of glue. A rip-off, it would seem, of Araldite. But then, a few days later, the car was on the pavement and where it once was stuck there was an injunction to get in touch with Apeldoorn Insurance.

Ten real green bottles can hang on a hoarding and fall to the ground one per day to announce the launch of a new apple drink, Appletiser. Actual bags of potato chips (or crisps as we say in the UK) can be attached to a site for sampling. Actual rolls of inferior adhesive wallpaper can be left to peel to demonstrate the superiority of the Dutch brand Perfax. A similar idea surfaced a few years earlier in the USA for a wallcovering firm. Wallpaper peels above the line 'It's time to go to Seabrook'.

Demonstration was called 'television's long suit'. Outdoor has demonstrated that no medium owns it exclusively. In Japan, to demonstrate Nichiba adhesive tape, ten thousand posters displayed in the underground corridors and on platforms were torn up one by one, by hand, and then pieced together using the product. Three Volkswagen Citi cars can be attached to a billboard to demonstrate the non-fading qualities of the

A real car on a billboard for an unreal fixative. When it fails there is a message to ring the insurance company. Centraal Beheer, The Netherlands, 1994, Agency: BSVR.

Crisp giveaways. The Netherlands, 1996.

Each week a new topical cartoon is painted on this Bombay site. The gentleman is John Major who is fighting the Maq Bull (or mad cow?). Amul Butter, India, 1996, Agency: D'Cunha and Associates.

Plaster Board

Covenant Healthcare, USA, 1995,
Agency: Birdsall Voss & Kloppenburg.

Band Aid, Canada, 1992,
Agency: Young & Rubicam.

Willie Rieser, Derma Plast,
Switzerland, 1975,
Agency: Advico-Delpire AG.

Actual plasters appear on billboards.
Mostly giant size. In Poland the upper
panel was addressed to English
speaking ex-pats. What to do in an
emergency? Help arrived a day or
two later with the answer on the
plaster – ABC Medicover.

The reverse process was used
in the USA by Covenant Healthcare.

In Canada Johnson & Johnson
demonstrated the sticking power
of a life-size Band Aid. Meanwhile
in Switzerland the poster artist
manages to depict before and after
in one telling visual for Derma Plast.

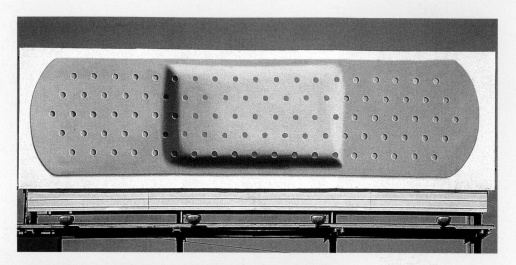

ABC Medicover, Poland, 1993,
Agency: Panintex/JWT.

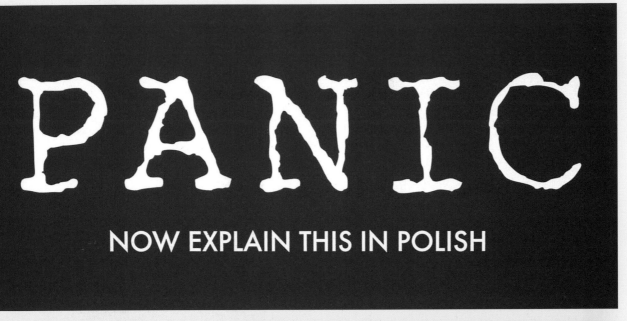

paintwork. Grass can grow on a site. Birds can be attracted by the careful placing of seeds. A bicycle can hang on a billboard to illustrate the Tour de France. Each day of the race the position of the bike and the accompanying message changed. Massive products can adorn the site. A real man can hang from the site, sit atop it or ride on a swing. An inflatable shark can smash through a billboard, fake bullet holes can pepper it, an insurance company can break one in two.

The shape and construction of the site can be brought into play. In the Fifties in Pittsburgh United Airlines were sold the use of a wall to advertise their inexpensive Florida vacations. Unfortunately in the middle there was a window and a fire escape ladder. The obvious solution was to paint only part of the wall. Instead they incorporated the window in the message and showed a lifesize mannequin in a bikini on the ladder and the line 'Why wait? Leave now'.

To demonstrate the discount it offers, Daffy's, a US retail chain, used up 30 per cent of the site to say 'this is what 70% looks like' and left the rest a gaping rectangle. A South African property company, Tower Lodge, used only the frame above a caption to show the actual residence behind. Qantas used a massive site to promote the wide open spaces of Australia. Prudential used the length of the board to show an arching rainbow and its end. The site can be wrapped in Christmas paper, held in by a belt. The column site can become to all intents and purposes a giant beer can.

During the launch month of a new unleaded petrol more and more greenery was added to the billboard until it was virtually covered with foliage. Wild birds were attracted with bird seed. Engen, South Africa,

1995, Agency: Tholet Sievers & Associates.

To prove the first half of the promise actual Golfs are hung up to dry at Johannesburg International Airport. VW Golf, South Africa, 1994, Agency: Ogilvy & Mather RS-TM.

Not simply a 3-D effect but an invitation to find out about the brand's lower fat promise. Carnation, Canada, 1993, Agency: McLaren: Lintas.

A supporting pole for a poster for a pickle becomes itself a giant pickle fork.

But to the purist the best solutions are those which bend no rule, ignore no constraint. Hiatt appreciated the fact at the end of the last century. 'To the ingenious designer there is a certain fascination in the strictness of these limits. The complexity of the problem always lures him, and gives him the appetite for experiment.'[20] The professional works within – and with – the limitations and honours the brief.

The brief comes first. Songwriter Sammy Cahn, when asked which came first, the words or the music, replied 'the phone call'.[21] The professional values the brief and the commercial *raison d'être*. Few works of art up to and including the Renaissance were born of the desire of the artist. 'J'aime les constraintes,' said Savignac, 'J'aime la difficulté.'[22] A similar sentence may have passed Michelangelo's lips on first looking at the barrel-vaulted Sistine ceiling, comforted by the fee of three thousand ducats.

Otis Shepard distinguishes between handicaps and limitations 'which help the craftsman to produce the most effective poster'.[23] Milton Glaser says 'make love to the problem'.[24] The journeyman artist will fight it, change it, bring in supporting aids. The task has been described by many designers but none so cogently as the man whose recent passing has robbed graphics of both a leading practitioner and a shrewd mind. Abram Games summed up the task as 'Maximum meaning. Minimum means.'[25] This is more than a description – it is a verbal illustration, a demonstration of his art.

A hole in the board to suggest there won't be one in your clothes budget. Daffy's, USA, Agency: Devito Verdi.

A real man on a swing. Swatch, Belgium, 1992, Agency: K.

Crashing through the billboard is a stitched nylon whale inflated with an electric fan. Marineland, USA, 1981, Agency: McCann-Erickson.

If the slogan doesn't give it away the shape does. Coca-Cola, Belgium, 1996, Agency: McCann-Erickson.

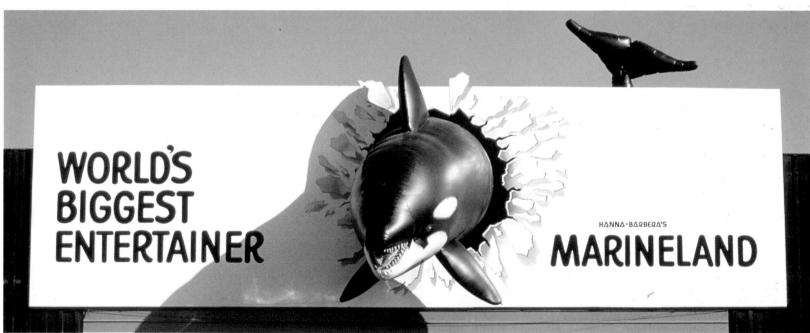

EN TOUR UNDER KANALEN

FØLG TOUR DE FRANCE I R1
SÅ SKER DER NOGET.

A Danish sports paper followed the Tour de France with a bicycle on a billboard. Each day adjusting the angle (of bike and message) and decorating it appropriately. 'A tour under the Channel', 'On your way to Paris' and 'Who wins on the Champs Elysees?'. BT, Denmark, 1995, Agency: BBDO A/S.

PÅ VEJ MOD PARIS

FØLG TOUR DE FRANCE I R1
SÅ SKER DER NOGET.

HVEM VINDER PÅ CHAMPS-ÉLYSÉES?

FØLG TOUR DE FRANCE I R1
SÅ SKER DER NOGET.

DRAMA I PYRENÆERNE

FØLG TOUR DE FRANCE I R1

HVEM ER STYRTET?

FØLG TOUR DE FRANCE I R1

HELLO - WELCOME TO ENGLAND

FØLG TOUR DE FRANCE I R1
SÅ SKER DER NOGET.

The strengths of outdoor

No other advertising medium is such a complex of paradoxes. Outdoor is old yet new. It is the oldest medium yet as we approach the millennium arguably the most dynamic. It is primitive and sophisticated. Flyposting of hand-produced bills still exists side by side with state-of-the-art technology. Paper and paste and digital and satellite cohabit. As do space and time – the one big, the other short – and change and permanence.

Outdoors This chapter examines what I believe are the major strengths of the outdoor medium – and the chief of these is the obvious but little appreciated fact of being outdoors. A poster message happens in the public arena where important things take place. Where the edict of the forthcoming execution of Louis XV was posted. And that too took place outdoors, in January 1793, in the Place de la Revolution. Outdoors, it is legitimate to speak loudly, to make the big gesture, to use the rhetoric of the street corner meeting inappropriate to the drawing room.

In 1952 a Milan gallery held a Savignac exhibition. The catalogue's introduction began 'Milan has the pleasure of presenting, in the great room of the Gallery of Modern Art, the *clamour* of Savignac's posters'. (my italics)

An outdoor ad is a public declaration which remains in place after it has been received. It is a form of 'direct communication with consumers where they live, work, play; where they drive and shop, where they commute and

Marlboro country – only this time it's South-East Asia. Marlboro, Malaysia, 1996, Agency: Leo Burnett.

Frozen motion. One of a series – and more dramatic when seen in sequence. Nike, USA, 1985, Agency: TBWA Chiat/Day.

This is nearer to the real Marlboro country – the Hollywood Hills. Marlboro, USA, 1980s, Agency: Leo Burnett.

congregate'. Ostensibly it is for everybody, that is for everybody to notice, though not necessarily take notice of. The content can select its specific audience but the medium itself is universal. An outdoor ad is seen by everybody – and each of us knows that everyone else is seeing it. Virtually everybody is outdoors every day: 233 million Americans, it is estimated. Moreover, their defences are down. The message can take advantage of this, bring the viewer up short, spring a question, plant a thought or suggest a purchase. There is not time to switch off, change channels or turn away. Similarly there is little time to commune except in such places as station concourses. At Waterloo Station a quarter of the people present do not actually catch a train!

Surprisingly there are very few examples of hoardings showing outdoor scenes. There is the occasional landscape (e.g. Marlboro) or sky (e.g. Carrefour) or clever use of the actual location (again Marlboro consistently does). Colorado shows its mountain ranges; California cheese depicts one made of cheeses; Utah, on a spectacular, displays actual trees and flowers; a car parks atop the Grand Canyon. An advertiser may use the site to improve the landscape by erecting a mural in front of an eyesore or building site. Indeed, the first official attempt in the USA to control the arbitrary or 'guerilla' posting of bills was a 'leased billposting station', a fence which in 1869 surrounded and hid the site of the new post office being built in City Hall Square, New York.

A drab roadcutting is hidden by a British Airways mural. South Africa, 1996, Agency: Partnership in Advertising.

What is freedom? asks the supermarket chain promoting its own brand products. Carrefour, France, 1976, Agency: RSCG.

On fait croire qu'un produit est meilleur simplement parce qu'il est plus cher.

C'est ça la liberté?

Carrefour.

As Phillips Russell was to observe some sixty years later:
A correctly designed and harmoniously executed poster is certainly a desirable screen for, and cheering relief from, straight and beautiful lines and faces of buildings which the brush of time and weather tends to change into a gaunt monotone.[1]
But very few advertisers have exploited the outdoor life as Pernod does ('They took to the streets') or identified themselves so completely with their location as Absolut vodka.

The use of the term 'street' today suggests that one is in touch. Streetwise. Street cred. Street smart. The news on the street. Perhaps it always has. 'What news on the Rialto?' asks Solanio of Salarino on a street in Venice. If Antony can tell Cleopatra that 'Tonight we'll wander through the streets and note the qualities of people', is it any wonder that Donna Karan, catering for today's lovers, states that DKNY 'is about the streets and if so, why aren't we out there on the streets?' And they are – on billboards, bus shelters and the sides of buses – contributing to what Emile Zola called, a century earlier in another place, 'la charme et la gaieté de la rue.'

Size The poster began big. This was its great attraction to advertisers and artists alike. Size and, of course, colour. A larger-than-life canvas. Brands began to flex their muscles. Advertisers could imply importance. The dominance of an immediate environment was transferred to the brand.

116 *Donna Karan identifies with New York. DKNY, USA, 1995.*

This effect was happening a century before Marshall McLuhan defined it: 'the medium is the message'. The *means* of the communication says more than the information it carries.

Bottles and packs became huge. Characters created around the brand or from the packaging were giants.

The poster began big in the USA. An observer in 1901 explained this. 'It's the country of big things.'[2] A visualization of America's immensity was reflected in its large paintings and enormous murals. During the Civil War a Union flag was depicted in a painting as if formed by a flaming sun and clouds across a vast sky. Copies were made and distributed to Unionist forces.

During World War Two the French-born Italian artist Achille Mauzan painted a poster thirty metres square for the National Loan. It was put up on the facades of all great public buildings. Architecture was the art Cassandre said he preferred to all others.

And when the poster was not big enough to show the actual dimensions of the product then the ingenuity of the poster artist would suggest size. A long-running poster campaign between the wars for Watney's beer featured a brick wall on which was painted in a legible but amateur hand, 'We want Watney's'. As most posters then were applied to walls the congruity of design and background gave the illusion of a very large advertisement.

In 1938 the advertising manager of Barnes Pianos borrowed the idea.

Pernod, UK, 1989, Agency: KMP Humphreys Bull & Barker Ltd.

When the logo is known, showing a part of it enlists the viewer's help in making it whole – and big. Here's the pick of the crop. Mickey made massive. Disneyland Paris, UK, 1996, Agency: Ogilvy & Mather.

had booked side panels on London's red buses and decided to photograph the piano against an identical red background. As he said, 'it looked as if Barnes had taken the whole bus'. (Later, of course, they could have.)

Cassandre's joyous invocations of sea and rail transport convey power and majesty by clever airbrushing of the image and geometric lettering, and emphasize size by choice of angle. Cassandre's visions soon became a common technique among American, British and Swedish transport companies. The Sascha Maurer design for the New Haven Railroad is imitation to the point of homage though I doubt if the master would have imposed so crass a headline.

Alternatively, clever cropping of the subject would permit the viewer to complete a mind picture. Orient Line's ship extends way beyond the confines of the picture and Disneyland Europe must be the home of the biggest Mickey Mouse ever (see p 117). Similarly, familiarity with the brand allows Coca-Cola India to show a mere fraction of the logo. This device ('less is more') works best when the image is solus. There are several examples of cropping (Fazer, Heineken, Campari, Viking Line) which extend the poster's size but note how the effect is lost when the repetition of the design in adjacent posters restricts expansion. Better to make two plus two equal five as Leupin does for Bata.

Posters became bigger to shout louder (outdoor is no place for reticence) but also to be seen at speed. 'Everything moves faster today', said poster

The logo cropping works less well when other ads are adjacent, even if they are your own. Viking Line, Finland, 1995.

Campari, Belgium, 1990s.

This chocolate advertiser restricts his signature to the first two letters - Ka or Fa of his names. Karl Fazer, Finland, 1995, Agency: SEK & Grey.

Heineken, The Netherlands, 1994.

Opposite: Angles, shadow, lines … impression of power and speed … yet all framed within the names of six companies and the designer and seven destinations! AM Cassandre, Nord Express, France, 1927.

With Cassandre, says Alain Weill, 'the machine found its herald'. Dramatic perspective heightened by the use of flat colour. The fearful symmetry broken only by the seagulls. Cassandre, French Lines, France, 1935.

Cropping again to suggest size. P&O, UK, 1960.

Sascha Maurer owes a debt to Cassandre. New Haven Railway, USA, 1936.

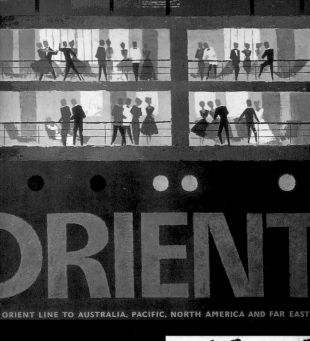

artist Joseph Binder (1898). 'We need the same speed to transmit the message effectively.'[3] As the number and speed of cars increased so too did the size of the hoarding. A twenty metre wide hamburger may adorn the freeway but to the advancing motorist at a hundred metres it is hamburger-size.

Sites grew in size and images extended beyond the sites. Skylines would be broken to attract attention. Whole walls would be painted. A corner site could be taken by one advertiser. And very often the grand was merely grandiose – when the idea was not as big as the board. The two monumental road-straddling signs from Bombay are certainly impressive. They are among the most expensive signage in India. But is the passer-by impressed by the advertiser ?

A big site can deliver impact. 'More impact than any newspaper ad', claims a US contractor from one of its sites. But what is impact if the message which is impacting is bland? Some advertisers are less concerned by this than others. Maybe they don't need a message but a dramatic shot of the brand or simply the logo to act as a reinforcement to a current, or a teaser to a forthcoming, print or TV campaign.

The fact that size can project authority can give an added importance to a local campaign making it appear national, especially when neighbouring ads promote national brands. Nevertheless, a big site really demands a big idea. As a London creative director said twenty years ago, 'big in size, the best posters are big in concept – warm, direct, friendly and simple.'[4] Would

Contractor Selvel leases this Bombay bridge from the government. It faces the heaviest traffic in the country. Visa, India, 1996, Agency: RK Swamy.

One of the sub-continent's largest hoardings, at Ahmedabad. Larsen & Toubro (an engineering group), India, 1996.

he so judge the dominant examples in this chapter? Would they fit his criteria?

But, as they say, size isn't everything. The biggest outdoor ads aren't necessarily the best. The growth of gigantesque sites may have peaked. In California, a big outdoor state, the medium has a 12 per cent share of advertising expenditure there compared with five per cent in the USA as a whole. However, though the medium is growing, the proportion of super sites has declined.

Location 'In outdoor advertising', says Jean Luc Decaux, 'the three most important factors are location, location, location.'[5] Hyperbole, of course, to reduce creativity of execution to, at best, fourth place. Nevertheless, for the media buyer and the creative team, knowing where the encounter between brand and consumer will take place is a tremendous asset. Today the contractor can provide reasonably accurate estimates of motor and pedestrian traffic, of opportunities to see the advertisement and can even, in the most recent development (POSTAR – see appendix), adjust the score according to the angle at which the site is approached. Additionally, there is the relevance of the site to the brand. Does it enhance the brand image? Is the passing traffic in the target market? Is the location capable of providing an opportunity to address a shopper about to make up his or her mind?

From the creative point of view, knowing where the consumer is can help

An outdoor contractor sells the medium. Naegele Outdoor, USA, 1989, Agency: Martin Williams.

The cropping dramatises the potential consumer's desire to move house. Prudential, 1993, Agency: WCRS.

target the message. This may be as widescale as producing different lines for different towns. Los Angeles is told by Campbells to eat its soup and by Hills coffee to perk up. But messages can be closer to home. Restaurants in the USA use billboards as directional signs. As do theme parks, zoos, racetracks, hotels and even one hospital: 'Last exit before by-pass'. An acupuncture clinic in London featured a map of the district and indicated its nearby location – with an actual giant pin. McDonalds tell subway passengers how few yards they need to walk for a Big Mac. Washington Mutual Bank placed an actual arrow on its billboard, pointing to a local landmark, above the line, 'Local Landmark. Local Bank', and arrowed the bank's name below. Ford chose a site in central London and next to a picture

of its car said to the approaching driver 'You're just 2½ gallons from Bristol in the new Ford Fiesta'. For the owner of a gas-guzzler this was a striking comparison.

But it would be too much to suggest that outdoor can specifically target discrete audiences. The upside of this is the medium's democracy. There is no restriction. No payment is required. There is no discrimination whether by age, race, gender, occupation or status. But if, to pursue the targeting analogy, the advertiser can't hit the bull or inner, there are compensating benefits. People not in the target market may influence those who are. Their circumstances may change. They may become target consumers because they grow older, move, become more affluent.

122

Two billboards from the 1980s addressed to Angelinos. Campbell's soup, 1977, Agency: BBDO. Hills Brothers' Coffee, 1971, Agency: Doyle Dane Bernbach.

The advertiser knows exactly where the viewer is and in what state. Welcome Break, UK, 1995, Agency: Young & Rubicam.

A neat variant using standard highway typeface – and knocking the competition. Daily Grill, USA, 1995, Agency: Ground Zero.

A directional sign and then a reminder. Louisiana Downs racecourse, USA, 1989, Agency: Philips Ramsey.

W Hesketh Lever, the founder of Lever Brothers, is credited with the famous line 'Half of the money I spend on advertising is wasted. The trouble is I don't know which half.'[6] But he did try to make it a science. For example, he would choose the exact sites where his enamel signs were to be displayed at railway stations. Would passengers be approaching? What could possibly obscure the sign? It's not known if he also considered what mood the passenger might be in. There is a case for making the message on a commuter platform for the train into work quite different from that for the return journey.

British Rail appreciated the mood of the car driver stuck in traffic. At notorious hold-up points it would take a billboard to state, 'If you were on a train you would be going too fast to read this poster.' It also appreciated that a poster on a platform and especially across the track need not be a five-second affair. In one Seventies classic it managed to list sixty locations with the journey times. It borrowed London Underground's map system and headlined the design, 'The Overground' (see p 125).

Other advertisers providing lengthy reading matter across tracks at rail and subway stations – e.g. insurance companies, holiday destinations, telecom services, magazines – are evidence of an understanding that outdoor is not a monolithic medium but, in expert hands, a medium of flexibility and variety.

Advertisers through the ages have capitalized upon the location of an

Four messages specific to each location. One-to-one communication.

Ford, UK, 1980s, Agency: Ogilvy & Mather.

Welcome to Dublin, Guinness, Ireland, 1996, Agency: HHCL.

British Rail, UK, 1977.

123

London Natural Health Clinic, UK, 1992.

Is the Wonderbra model really standing at this bus stop? So it seems. In reality the shot was taken at the precise location. Eva was photographed in a Paris hotel. The two images were married. Voilà. Gossard, UK, 1996, Agency: TBWA.

Work in progress, right. Eva's double.

THE ONE AND ONLY Wonderbra

individual site to make a point. Guinness chose to associate their campaign (Guinness for strength) with the demolition of the old Waterloo Bridge. Wonderbra posed their model against a photograph of the view behind a specific bus shelter. Duracell batteries have a long-running campaign featuring toy rabbits. They could not resist tying it in with Warren Street underground station.

Permanence An advertising message could become unstuck when the poster couldn't. There are cases of advertisements remaining in place long past their sell-by date. Woodrow Wilson's election posters of 1916 – 'He kept us out of the war' – were still up when he declared war the following year.

Advertisers were keen to retain certain sites. They became landmarks. 'Turn right by the Oxo poster'. Posters became fixed in the memory. Long after the tenant of the site changed, the image remained.

There is this strange impression of permanence. It is given tangible form when in a French village one sees a faded painted Dubonnet sign or in England, still screwed to the wall, an enamel sign for Oxo.

Enamel signs 'implied that not only the manufacturer and his product, but also the advertised claims would last forever'.[7] But if today's outdoor ad is not that permanent (and the average life of a billboard site in the UK is only two years) it remains displayed and visible every hour of the day and, increasingly, night and its impact and involving message can keep it in the

125

An appropriately named subway station is made to tie in with the campaign character for the long-lasting battery. Duracell, UK, 1995, Agency: Ogilvy & Mather.

Intercity poster, BR, UK, 1970s.

On the main road out of town the local beer says farewell and allows the bottle itself to complete the message. Newcastle Brown Ale, UK, 1995, Agency: CDP.

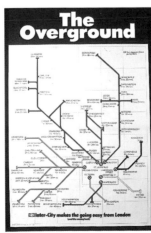

memory. Certainly the advertising one remembers from childhood is more often than not outdoor ads. Posters were part of growing up. The relative constancy of a poster's presence affords a higher viewing frequency than other media. People pass the same site repeatedly.

The medium can somehow carry a sense of heritage. The brand becomes part of the environment, 'owns the space' and yet takes nourishment from it. The outline bull on the Spanish hill for Osborne (see pp 40–1) dominates the landscape and stays in the mind. The Tuborg poster dates from the beginning of the century. I saw it posted again recently in Copenhagen. I don't expect the Danish brewer re-runs old press ads.

Continuity contributes to the sense of permanence. Citylights and illuminated billboards permit twenty-four hour visibility. But in the 1870s Barnum, then America's most extensive outdoor advertiser, achieved the same effect with a big gaslit sign which illuminated Broadway for several blocks.

In 1891 the great white way (as Broadway became known) was initiated with the first electric sign on the site of what was to become the Flatiron building. Early advertisers were Heinz, White Rock water and Wrigley. One painted sign read, 'Buy houses on Long Island', and listed some of its attractions – a beach, two hotels, a band and Brocks fireworks. Not long afterwards, of course, the site could have provided a sample of the last. For in 1910, close by in Herald Square, on the roof of the Hotel Normandie, the

126

A new version of the brand message of an old classic. Tuborg, Denmark, 1996, Agency: McCann-Erickson.

Classic turn-of-the-century poster still reproduced on Copenhagen hoardings. No bottle is shown and the viewer makes the connection. Tuborg, Denmark, last seen 1994.

Edison company erected a moving chariot race created with twenty thousand bulbs beneath the lighted message 'Leaders of the world at your service. Light, heat and power.' (Note how in both America and Europe inventions and advances are tied to images of the past rather than visions of the future.) Subsequently, the message area was occupied by advertisers; Armour, Remington, Prudential, NCR, Quaker Oats among them. Names not unknown today.

The sense of permanence is reinforced if the basic advertising message remains the same. Variations can be played but the theme is constant. The classic posters are nearly always part of classic campaigns: Bovril, Dubonnet, Nicolas, Guinness, Volkswagen.

An enduring advertiser but always in touch. Kinetic art adopted by the ecelectic Cassandre, Nicolas, France, 1935.

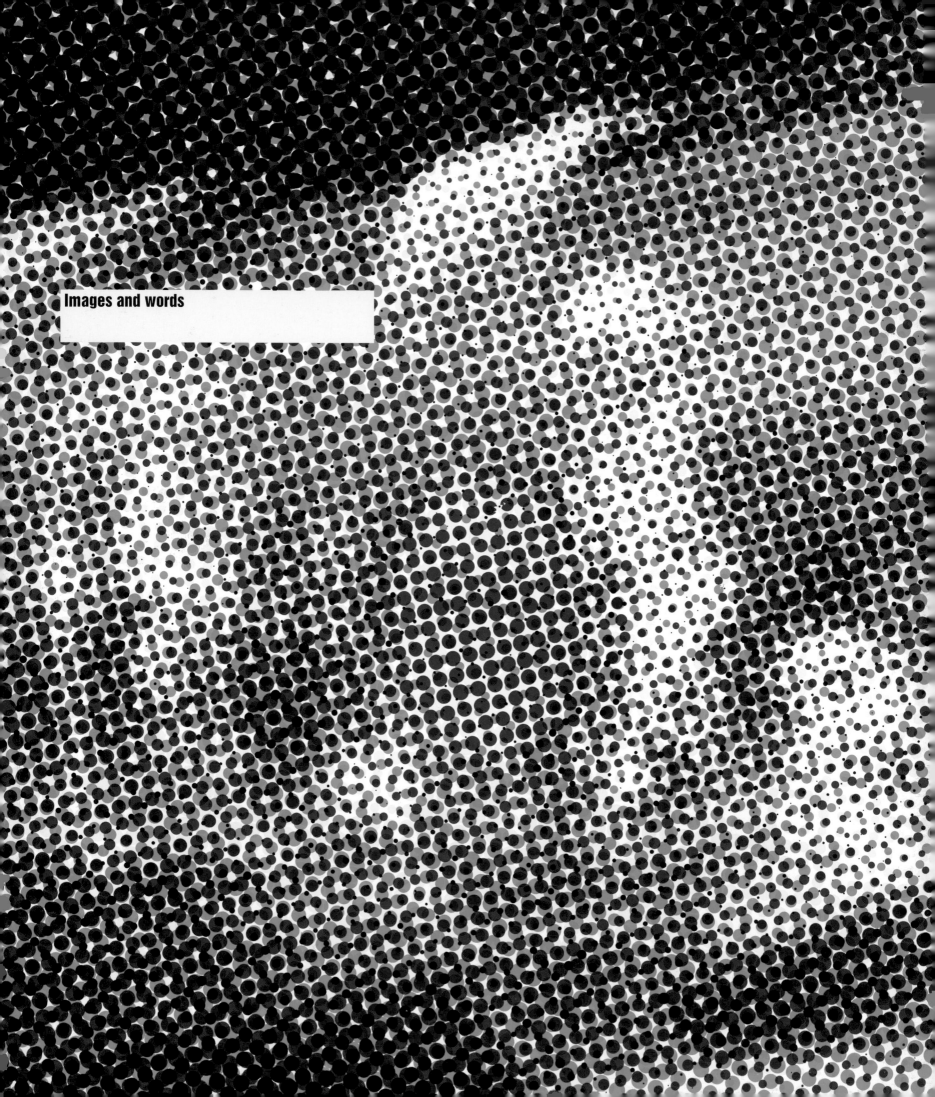

Images and words

The fashionable media commentator who forecasts the 'death of the word' may be puzzled by contemporary outdoor advertising. Certainly in North America and Western Europe the image has not triumphed despite the growth of visual literacy. Is it a last ditch stand, a throw back, evidence of a resistance to change by a traditional medium? I believe it is none of these things. Text-dominant outdoor ads sometimes reflect the narrative of a television commercial – or, more frequently, complement it. Often the support poster either portrays a shot of the pack or a still from the commercial and adds a comment, or engages in dialogue, even dispensing with image entirely. As we have seen, certain locations are suitable for the reading of text. (At a Dallas street crossing a sign read 'This light takes

forever. So you might as well read this billboard'.) However, a wall newspaper the medium is not. And today's, possibly temporary, word-led tendency is a far cry from the 'golden age' of poster design (whenever that was) or indeed, the less glorious years when image was all. Here is Abram Games describing the early Thirties scene.

…this thrilling visual medium was made dull and lifeless by those who regarded it as a coloured picture with lettering imposed. It was usual at that time for 'posters' to be 'designed' without a definite subject let alone a client in mind. Appropriate lettering was added in a convenient blank space once a client could be found to buy the poster. A picture of a prepared table, for instance, might be sold and lettered for a

'Bubbles' by Sir John Millais appropriated by the advertiser – and where else would you put the brand name? Pears, UK, 1887.

manufacturer of furniture, foodstuffs, linen or crockery. It made no difference to the artist or seller as long as he was paid.[1]

What Games describes is not dissimilar from the situation at the modern poster's birth. Art was frequently bought 'off the peg' from either an established or a journeyman artist, possibly with one eye on the comparatively lucrative market.

Sir John Millais painted his grandson blowing soap bubbles. Pears' Soap purchased 'Bubbles' and added the brand name. Furore enlivened the art world. Millais' son, however, was more conciliatory, hoping that the ad would 'raise the character of our illustrated advertisements' and 'lead to the final extinction of such atrocious vulgarities as now offend the eye at every turn'.[2]

Pears' Soap in 1884 ran a press ad featuring the celebrated actress Lily Langtry. Since using the brand, 'I have discarded all others', she wrote in her own handwriting which was copied by a forger to her considerable financial discomfiture. The event made the papers and *Punch* magazine published a cartoon featuring a grubby tramp writing a similar testimonial. Pears, with the permission of *Punch*, again added their name and reprinted it as a handbill. In 1896 an American advertiser appropriated the design and re-drew it for their brand ABC lager.

The link between picture and brand was often as tenuous as Abram Games suggested. A significant Dutch Impressionist George Hendrik Breitner gave the manufacturer of Delft Salad Oil permission to use his painting of

Full circle? *Pears use a Punch cartoon which itself is a caricature of a Pears advertisement.* **Harry Furness, Pears, UK, c1895.**

Not quite – *American Brewing Company, USA, c1896.*

two cart horses on a building site. A message and the brand name were printed in the frame.

A Japanese historian of his country's advertising says of the posters produced between 1870 and 1930 that they were essentially 'developed by the addition of a client's advertising words to the decorative pictures of beautiful women'.[3] This is Chéret territory and the 'pretty girl mania' Shepard spoke of. If the girl is attractive then so – one hopes – is the poster… but the brand?

The Beggarstaffs exhibited posters at an exhibition in 1894 for products of an imaginary company they called Nobody, hoping that an appropriate manufacturer would purchase the designs for Nobody's Candles, Nobody's Pianos, Nobody's Blue, etc. (Of course, if they couldn't find a buyer they could turn the last one into the title of a song for piano accompaniment.)

The famous John Hassall design 'Skegness is *so* bracing' also began life as an orphan. The oil painting was bought for twelve pounds by the Great Northern Railway and later acquired by the town. Hassall was made a freeman of Skegness in 1934, an event which prompted his first visit. But then he had not specifically designed it for Skegness or GNR or anyone. Ironically, that is precisely what makes it stand out from the usual beach scenes, happy families and bathing belles.

Contemporary and traditional artistic themes were dragooned into service. In the USA a patriotic mural in the Capitol building in Washington

132

'Decorative pictures of beautiful women'… part of the timeless quality of the brand's advertising. Shiseido, Japan, 1925.

John Hassall. Originally used by the Great Northern Railway, UK, 1908. Subsequently adopted (illustrated) by the town itself. The design was simplified, clouds departed the blue sky and a hand breaks the frame.

was adapted as a poster featuring a farmer driving a McCormick reaper. Classical, patriotic, historic and other portentous images were made to sell bicycles, railways, patent medicines, foods, etc. An image that is anybody's is nobody's unless the advertiser manages to lock in the brand name and the brand promise. Even then, if similar images are decorating the walls, often by the same artist, exclusivity and effectiveness are diminished.

The pictorial element was somehow separate. And this had a detrimental effect on advertising, if not art, for it moved the poster nearer to art than applied art. The well-known popular images at the turn of the century, especially in Britain, which adorn the poster books are appreciated for their aesthetics. The art gallery has moved to the street but later when the posters were displayed in the gallery something of the street came with them – the need for simplicity and focus and planes of flat colour in order to attract the passing eye – but not the actual commerce of the street.

Art as a separate entity within a commercial context endured longer in Britain than France. Some major advertisers could of course justify displaying paintings, acting almost as patrons of both young and proven talent, since what they painted were either locations, served by the railway or the motor car, or scenes of activity in the goods yards or docks.

Frank Pick at London Underground (from 1908) and Jack Beddington at Shell (from 1923) chose emerging and established artists to paint scenes. Paul Nash, Graham Sutherland, Ben Nicholson, Frank Brangwyn, Barnett

The brand provides a frame in which the artist interprets a destination as he or she sees it. Edwin Calligan, Llangollen, Shell, UK, 1933.

Graham Sutherland, Brimham Rock, Shell, UK, 1932.

133

PLAS NEWYDD LLANGOLLEN   EDWIN CALLIGAN

Freedman and others, though they occasionally adopted its techniques, did not move the poster forward. That was left to lesser-known graphic designers – E McKnight Kauffer, Tom Gentleman, Tom Purvis, Eckersley-Lombers – who, integrating text and image, achieved far more impact. The masters of the medium on both sides of the English Channel were expressing the brand promise through their art, not merely appending their art to a brand name.

Compare the average scenic view with Cassandre's Étoile du Nord (1927) 'which combines a feeling for the new technology and a complete faith in its function'.[4] Posters may have turned the street into an art gallery but in this gallery people are on the move and the artist has to grab attention with movement of his own, colour and impactful lettering.

A poster should be 'bold, simple, striking', demands Paul Rand.[5] 'There is no place', said Savignac, 'for an interplay of tone, for refinement or subtle suggestion. In the midst of the colour, light and movement of the street these things are invisible.'[6]

The poster is not an illustration as in the press where it accompanies the text. In a poster the visual delivers the message. Carlu calls it the 'graphic expression of the idea', although 'explosion' might be a better word.

Realistic paintings of the product and the user – so popular in the USA – and then photography with its mechanical perfection lack the impact which simple lines, simple shapes and flat colour can achieve. This Purvis

134 *Simple, disciplined design with a daring presentation of the product. Ludwig Hohlwein, Kehl, Germany, 1908.*

Sparse detail, bold colours and artistic freedom with the logo. Tom Purvis, Shell, UK, 1928.

demonstrates omitting any detail he considers irrelevant. See too the Kaloderma design of Jupp Wiertz. Instantly assimilated are the swathes of colour – or, in the case of Hohlwein, swatches of cloth.

Silk screen printing, inexpensive and suitable for short print runs, proved an ideal poster medium encouraging the use of 'simple, bold, striking' images.

Dramatic simplicity is key. Emphasis must be on the most important item. And the design and the brand must be inextricably linked.

To return to the question 'Is Brand Evident?',[8] can you tell when you see it – and afterwards – whom or what the ad is for? Or, to put it another way, 'who is the hero?' If the brand isn't the hero what's going on? Branding isn't simply ensuring that the brand name is writ large, though sometimes the minimalist logo becomes perverse, but that the totality of the design is conveying the character of the brand, that the effect is coherent. The *Economist* campaign (see p 175) is entirely coherent. There is no doubt who is the hero. Identity is achieved not simply by the colour scheme (The *Economist* is red and white) but by the typeface and especially the tone of voice. The magazine treats the viewer with respect. Also coherent was the classic Volkswagen Beetle campaign. Again the design and typeface were consistent but note how identity is achieved; throughout this campaign there was no slogan or baseline – or a massive logo.

Early posters made little use of the logo. This is not to say that the brand

Power – even without the engine. The rails point the eye to the horizon and the North Star. Again note the framing text. Cassandre, L'Étoile du Nord, France, 1927.

Flat colour and elegance. Jupp Wiertz, Kaloderma, Germany, 1927.

name is not registered but there is little attempt either to represent the pack or logo or to maintain consistency of lettering across different executions. It was not till after World War Two that poster artists truly recognized that the logo offered great potential for impressing the brand name upon the passer-by. They removed it from the pack, gave it momentum and size, distorted it, and by playing with it made it work. See how Leupin emphasizes excitement for Bata and Suze.

This is not to say that earlier designers ignored the brand name as an element in the design over and above a mere brand identification. Names were often integrated into the designs, for example, but the artists were allowed to letter them as they wished. Notice in Mucha's design for Job

cigarette papers how the large name at the top differs in form (not to mention size) from the logo on the actual pack in the lady's hand. In the accompanying design the name is treated in yet another way.

This was the case also with Shell, for example in Jean d'Ylen's design. Shell, otherwise graphically aware, were not in the vanguard of corporate identity, the introduction and maintenance of a house style, as were AEG in Germany, Olivetti in Italy and the Container Corporation of America. It was not until the Fifties that the pioneering work of designers such as Hans Schleger and FHK Henrion became recognized.

Today no corporate identity manual or company legal department would tolerate d'Ylen's artistic licence. Conversely, if the logo is consistently

'The magic is in the product' said Bill Bernbach, who, with Helmut Krone and Julian Koenig, created a campaign which changed not only car advertising but advertising itself. A promise in every ad. And branded.

Volkswagen, USA, 1960–72, Agency: Doyle Dane Bernbach.

Note the variants in the Job and Shell logos. Alphonse Mucha, Job cigarette papers, France, 1896.

Alphonse Mucha, Job cigarette papers, France, 1898.

Jean d'Ylen, Shell, UK, c1925

Jean d'Ylen, Shell, UK, c1925

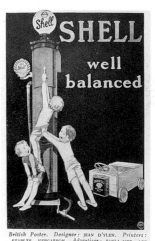

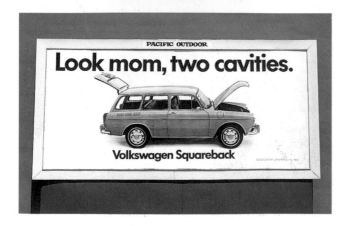

maintained, then it becomes an instant symbol for the brand, visual shorthand. It can still perform tricks – provided that it does not change its form. The famous McDonalds' M is made to carry three extra meanings in the Swedish street sign.

A logo becomes a valuable property. As with literal properties, they should increase in value if properly maintained. Cutty Sark's distinctive lettering was used to project the message 'Happy Holiday'. Nothing else appeared on the huge board but those two words on the yellow background equalled four. Marmite performs a similar trick, adding a sound dimension, relabelling their jar on the poster 'My mate'.

Though logos did not feature hugely in early designs, packs themselves often did – and after all the pack carried the logo. It happens most frequently in American posters: for example, Armour's meat extract, Quaker Wheat Berries, Petitjohns Breakfast Food and American Brewing Company.

Later on the pack featured more predominantly in the design without being a simple pack shot. The Bovril jar played a role as did the ink bottle in Cappiello's design and in Savignac's noted Bel Paese composition (see p 140).

Occasionally and memorably a collection of packs or bottles became a character for the brand, e.g. Lampo Benzine and the Holsten can man. Trade figures became popular – Sandeman, Johnny Walker, Yardley's Lavender girl, the Michelin man, the Bisto kids, Aunt Jemima, etc.

In medieval signs the letters are an integrated part of the work.

3M? No – four. McDonalds', Sweden, 1992, Agency: Rönneberg McCann.

This dates from around 1890 though the trade mark was registered in 1877. Quaker, USA, 1890.

Pettijohn's, USA, c1890.

Leonetto Cappiello, Inchiostri Bo, 1921.

A two word message conveying also a one word brand name. Marmite, UK, 1995, Agency: Ogilvy & Mather.

137

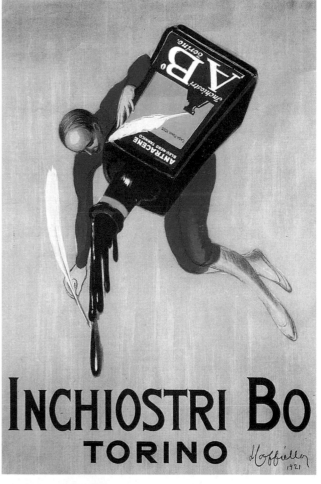

The Story of 'O'

The creative challenge is to fuse image and text. When an image is part of that text – albeit just a letter – fusion is easier.

(See also page 151)

Bern Health Authority, Switzerland, 1995.

Interflora, UK, 1994, Agency: Ammirati Puris Lintas.

Red Label Tea, Saudi Arabia, 1996, Agency: Tihama Mona International.

Opposite: Leonetto Cappiello, Oxo, UK, 1920s.

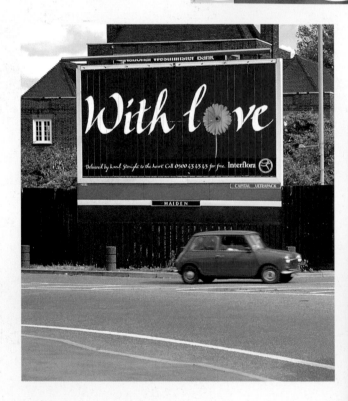

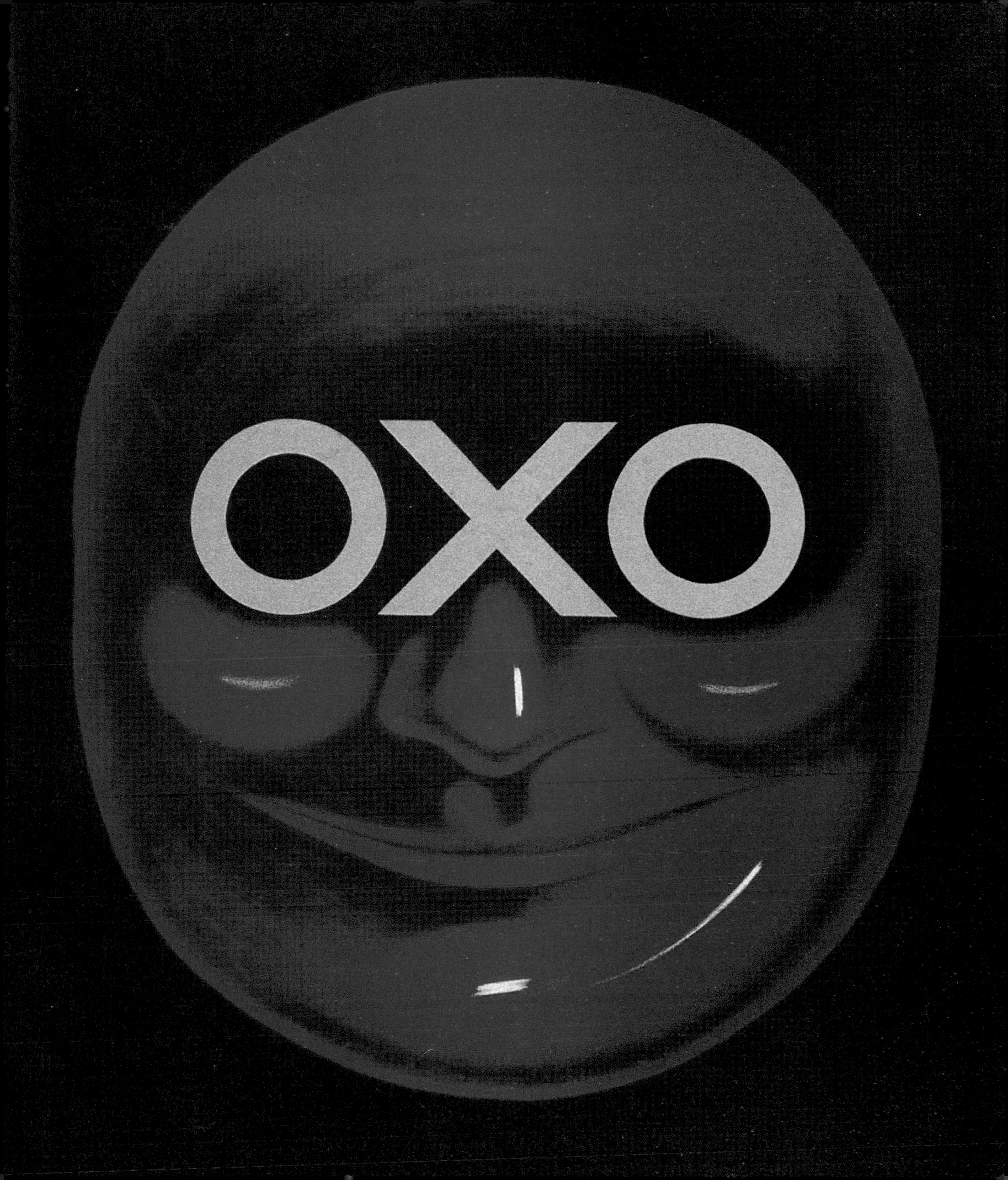
OXO

The earliest poster artists, however, regarded lettering as no more than either a necessary but less significant item of the design or a decorative element. Early designs reflected the whim of the artist or the lettering or type style of the period. It took some while to recognize that type could forge identity. Branding demanded consistency. Some brands decided enough was enough and the type style changes hardly at all over the generations (e.g. St Bruno, Lyon's Tea, Camp).

The letters could form the image. Georges Braque had incorporated letters: contemporary typefaces suggested reality. Poster artists, however, went further using type not merely to communicate the name of the brand or a promise but as a dynamic means of illustrating that promise. The look of the letters, their size, tone and, above all, arrangement could all work to reinforce the thrust of the advertiser's message. The what and how of the communication process were becoming fused. Note, for example, Cassandre's Nord Express and his Dubo… Dubon… Dubonnet, McKnight Kauffer's lubrication by Shell and Ashley Havinden's Eno's design. Leupin we have already noted (Suze and Bata) but his Swiss colleagues also encourage the lettering to work. Look especially at Orio Galli's Café Moretto. The Dutch Heineken design makes the brand make a smile.

Conversely, type can be used in complex and changing forms within one design, as for example the compelling Autoglass billboard. Even more words appear on the adjacent poster for Red Stripe, an ethnic beer.

The two street urchins uncharacteristically dressed up and indoors. Will Owen, Bisto, 1930s.

Raymond Savignac, Bel Paese, France, c1950.

Orio Galli, Café Moretto, Switzerland, 1970.

'One of the icons of the period' (Richard Hollis). AM Cassandre, Dubonnet, France, 1932.

Autoglass, UK, 1995, Agency: BMP DDB.

Red Stripe, UK, 1996, Agency: BST BDDP.

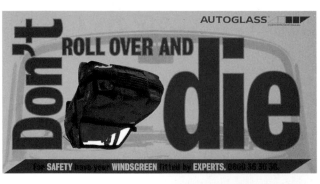

But maybe the purist believes that the best poster design contains no words. Communicating by the visual alone is the supreme test. The addition of words which contribute nothing to the essential message is a belt-and-braces exercise. Returning to the Heineken face, what purpose would such a line serve: 'Heineken brings a smile to your lips and lights up your eyes'? Does the Kub bouillon design want for a verbal message? Similarly look at the Elbeo sock advertisement. It does not need a line such as 'Ties for your feet'. The connection is already made visually. An Israeli safe sex poster superimposes a lifebuoy on the ring of a condom. The caption 'Life Saver' is tautologous. Less is more. Too often words are added because the image has failed to deliver, as we saw in the Buick Riviera ad (see p 95).

The viewer who decodes, who participates in the message-*making*, is more likely to remember or 'own' the message. Though whether he or she always understands the design is another matter.

The Micra car has succeeded with minimalist design and very few words. The powerful US anti-drug image needs no accompanying injunction. Note how Leupin (again) manages to convey without any words, other than those contained within the product, two separate thoughts for two newspapers – the global coverage of *Weltwoche* (see p 142) and the every morning habit of the *Tribune* (see p 78). The Swiss are good at this.

As are the Japanese who have a tradition of visual supremacy and people are visually oriented, trained to appreciate the shape as well as the

*Frans Mettes, Heineken,
The Netherlands, 1953.*

*The brand has to solve the identical
problem faced by Bovril and
Oxo – to identify the product with
its origin. Leonetto Cappiello, Kub,
France, 1931.*

*Elbeo, Germany, 1992,
Agency: RG Weismeier.*

Advertising Council, USA, 1990s.

meaning of the characters. Until recently this meant that copywriting was regarded as a supplementary job. One award-winning art director asserts, 'I put an idea forward but I don't carry it out and the words don't interest me. I sometimes remove them.'[9] (Mind you, I've worked with one or two art directors like that.)

Games believed that 'lettering must work equally with the design and not be merely an added afterthought. If need be lettering alone should be the basis of the idea.' That is certainly the case with 'schreibmaschinen' with the brand name at its heart. Games added a necessary caveat: 'Text should be reduced to a minimum in order to accentuate its significance.'[10]

The Japanese view is slightly different. A leading art director Takashi

Nakahata is worth quoting at length:

> The text does not fundamentally change the visual impact, but it goes deeper into the meaning. If you compare it to an accessory, it would be the handle of a cup, or a saucepan. It enables contact to be made, and, therefore, access to what is human. In other words, the image is to look at and the words attract the audience. After all, it's the same relationship as exists in music between the melody and the word. You enjoy the former, but are moved by the 'story.'[11]

Takashi would probably be bemused by some of the word-dominated outdoor ads in Britain. Why should a breakfast cereal resort to showing a sentence 'Stay Trim. Lift a Spoon Every Morning'? Or an airline commanding

The brand emerging from the product. IBM Typewriters, Germany, 1978, Agency: GGK.

Herbert Leupin, Die Weltwoche, Switzerland, 1949.

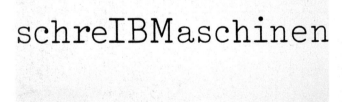

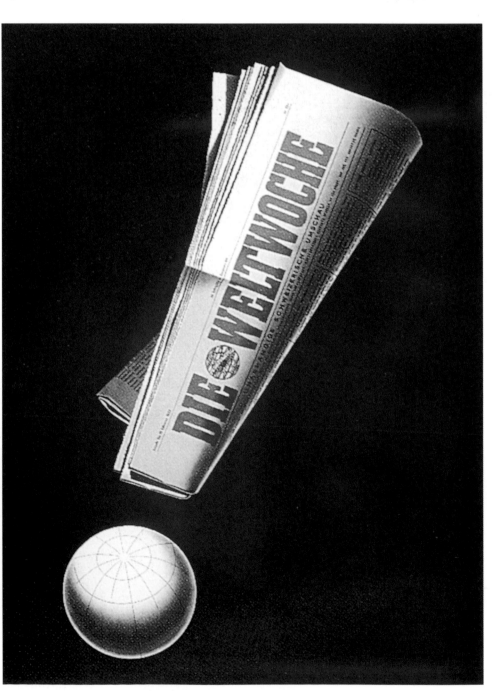

'Vote With Your Backside'? Or the *Economist* never showing the product in its advertising? But his appreciation of music might allow him to be moved by the lyrics of Frère Swatch.

Words obviously have played a major part in poster successes. Many slogans were born outdoors. Others were given an airing. 'It floats', 'Guinness is Good for You', 'I'd walk a mile for a Camel', 'We want Watney's', 'Drinkapintamilkaday', 'You can be sure of Shell'.

To stay in the memory the slogan needs, above all, to be short and preferably simple. Rhyme helps. As do rhythm, alliteration and assonance. A pun may help (see later) and if it is integrated into the design so much the better.

Integration of image and word is harder to achieve than many of advertising's creative people believe. It is more than mere linkage. It is *fusion*. Milton Glaser decrees that a true poster will not allow you to remove one element without damaging the design – and the effect.

Examine the deceptively simple design for Martini Vermouth by Hans Schleger (Zero). The proposition is that Martini is the genuine Italian vermouth for the drink gin and Italian. The copy line reduces the thought to five words ('With gin this is It'). The visual combines bottle and glass. Words and text are integrated.

The vast majority of today's outdoor ads don't fuse but link. Often the link is ingenious (for example, the Triumph TR7 on p 86). The majority of

Weetabix, UK, 1995, Agency: Lowe Howard-Spink.

National Milk Publicity Council, UK, 1958, Agency: Mather & Crowther (subsequently Ogilvy & Mather).

Allegedly the slogan was uttered by a man who cadged a Camel from a sign painter at work on a billboard. The sign painter passed the line on. RJ Reynolds, Camel, USA, 1921.

Swatch, Belgium, 1992, Agency: K.

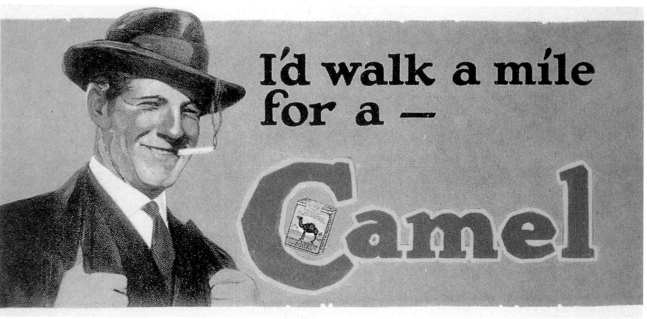

designs are images to which a thought is linked. (This does not necessarily mean that the visual idea came first.) To a shot of a fast-moving car is added the line 'Fast relief from stress'. A dozen other lines could accompany it. KFC offer a variety of short order lines which accompany their standard offerings rather like condiments (e.g. 'Best legs in town'). This is a very American format. It can sink to the banal and politically incorrect (as with Alcoa's 'Wife Saver' ad for aluminium foil).

However, when there is a tension between the words and image – as in 'Hip Flask' which appropriately celebrates the rebirth of the Thermos – the effect is more powerful. The caption to the shot of the soldier opening his parcel is poignant and to the point for the Finnish Post Office. To call the

restaurant at the Alcatraz theme park 'the original Hard Rock Cafe' is witty. As is the idea of stating that the Duracell bunny is for life rather than just Christmas. So too were most of the VW comments, e.g. 'It makes your car look bigger' for the Beetle and 'Mass Transit' accompanying the shot of nuns in a minibus.

Nevertheless, few,if any, of these examples would pass the Glaser fusion test. Note, however, how the captions 'Göteborg' and 'Malmo' unite with the photograph of the grandfather and boy to communicate the idea of quickly and cheaply uniting them through SJ Airlines. Another airline BOAC, forerunner of BA, based a campaign for its VC10 on the comfort of the seat. One in the series summed up the offering in the word 'Unfold' and shaped

144 *Hans Schleger (Zero), Martini, UK, 1948, Agency: WS Crawford.*

SJ Airways, Sweden, 1990, Agency: Rönnberg & Co.

'At least there's the Post Office,' says a comforted serviceman. Finnish Postal Authority, Finland, 1995, Agency: Paltemaa Huttenen Santala.

the word to suggest the aircraft. Similarly a Swiss Coca-Cola design has the word 'delicious' lettered in the shape of a Coke bottle. Fifty years before, Spratts animal feed shaped the brand name to resemble a dog or a cat.

For *Il Giorno* Savignac makes the newspaper a window. Games makes the *Financial Times* become a trouser leg. And for many people the isle of Jersey still means holidays in the sun, lounging in the J deck chair. Hervé Morvan uses cigarettes and the barest silhouette of a dancer to convey the Spanish association of Gitanes. Savignac, again, fused cow and soap to register for all time the milk content of Monsavon. Leupin puts one word at the centre of his design to support the reinvigorating power of Coca-Cola.

Alexandre Alexeieff in 1928 was commissioned to portray the quality of the catering on the London North Eastern Railway. He shows no train but a shadowy diner at a table on the rails. The caption 'Dine on the LNER' is necessary only to brand, not to explain. Sometimes, however, the caption works against the picture to create not tension but confusion (see the Lewitt-Him design for American Overseas Airlines). And sometimes the fusion becomes too tight.

An immediately comprehensible Guinness fusion is the dartboard poster revealing a glass of the stout at the high point of the board. Guinness over the years have experimented with various images, for example having a glass of the product take the place of the old gasometer overlooking the Oval cricket ground or appear within the massive Cheddar Gorge. But, as

145

Abram Games, Financial Times, *UK, 1951.*

Coca-Cola, USA, 1970s, Agency: McCann Erickson.

Abram Games, Jersey, UK, 1958.

Alexandre Alexeieff, LNER, UK, 1928.

BOAC (subsequently BA), UK, 1967, Agency: Garland Compton (subsequently Saatchi & Saatchi).

A classic branding for a dog food, which also featured on enamels. Max Field-Bush, Spillers, UK, 1936.

The master of the visual pun sold his first poster at the age of 41. This was it. Raymond Savignac, Monsavon, France, 1949.

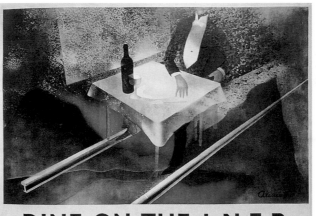

puns go, the dartboard is double top – i.e. both elements are relevant, as both are key constituents of any good public house.

By the same token, the little known design for the Wimbledon tournament is also an appropriate pun. A tennis ball made of grass is no fanciful conceit, it shouts *lawn* tennis. Both elements of a pun should be relevant to the brand. When a cigarette manufacturer adorned the walls with 'Players Please' he communicated both a claim and a request; the message went from the wall to the tobacconist's shop. When Band Aid show cartoon characters on their product they are entitled to say 'We're stuck on kids'. When McDonalds turn their M ninety degrees to form the Z in pizza the two thoughts are communicated simultaneously. As when a Canadian outdoor

contractor uses one of its boards to announce, 'People read as they go buy'.

But commonly a punning headline works at only one level. The intention is either to lure the viewer into thinking of one thing and then realizing it refers to something else or to puzzle the viewer into making a connection between the brand and the seemingly unrelated message. So 'learn to hold it till you get to the can' leads to a baseline: 'Don't litter'. 'Shock Therapy' is seen to refer to an auto supply company's servicing of shock absorbers. 'Relieves gas pains' is – you guessed it – for the VW Beetle. 'We can't go on seeing each other like this', says a man to a woman in a cinema-style scene typical except for the fact that both are wearing two pairs of spectacles. Clearly they need bifocals.

146 *This striking Dali-esque image is not really helped by the slogan. Lewitt-Him, American Overseas Airlines, UK, 1948.*

Lawn Tennis Association, UK, originally designed 1957, Agency: Charles Barker.

A brilliant fusion. Notice the way the advertiser re-introduces the idea of 'good for you'. Guinness, UK, 1977, Agency: J Walter Thompson.

A legitimate pun, Band Aid, Canada, 1992, Agency: Young & Rubicam.

Hook Outdoor Advertising, Canada, 1993, Agency: Hook Outdoor Advertising.

On rare occasions the pun combines two languages. 'Ménage Artois' is an Australian ad for Stella. 'Pomme çi. Pomme ça,' a German ad for French apples. Clever – but do they say anything, apart that is from, 'hey I'm smart'? Perrier have been doing this in the UK far more tellingly by using the word *eau* within English words (e.g. N'eau calories, H2 Eau). Interestingly in Belgium the brand uses a visual pun. A motorist stopped by the police blows up a balloon which becomes the shape of the Perrier bottle.

Visual or verbal, the good pun is a legitimate means of achieving what all outdoor ads must attempt to achieve, namely a fusion. However, the ideal fusion is not of word with word, or picture with picture but of text with image.

To adapt the question asked of Sammy Cahn, which comes first the words or the picture? One designer has no doubt: assume that, 'the people who see it cannot, or at least will not, read it'. Since a poster must work quickly the image must lead the attack or tackle the passer-by single-handed.

There are some brilliant examples of images doing it if not alone, then with no more than the brand name or logo (e.g. Bally). Van Nelle's coffee conveys strength by means of seven cups and three shadows.

However, most poster artists would seem to agree that the task of the visual is to deliver the message which is then immediately reinforced by the (minimal) text. In boxing terms it's a one-two. But, of course, part of that initial punch comprises the shape, if not the meaning, of the text. Nakahata, as we saw, believes that text reinforces, 'goes deeper into the medium'.[12]

VW, USA, 1963, Agency: Doyle Dane Bernbach.

French apples, Germany, 1994.

Environmental agency, Canada, 1992, Agency: Harrod & Mirlin.

Stella Artois, Australia, 1994, Agency: Clemenger (Perth).

Abram Games's favourite of all his posters was the 1942 'Your talk may kill your comrades.'[13] The initial impact is of a mouth from which emanates a spiral, ending in the impaling of three servicemen. Next, the eye is drawn to the words, 'Talk may kill', then the whole line.

The picture of the man on the floating Bovril jar communicates something intriguing and presumably beneficial, not to mention the brand name. The words reinforce, illuminate the meaning.

Cassandre would begin with the text – the centre of the composition. 'It is around the text that the design should turn, not the reverse.'[14] Probably his best known design proves the point – 'Dubo… Dubon… Dubonnet'.

I had designed a little Parisian sitting at a table, drinking Dubonnet. I lettered as far as 'Dubo' – when the telephone rang, and I had to go out to see a client. When I came back I saw 'Dubo' (*du beau*) – I had the idea… tore up my almost finished design and started anew. That's the origin of 'Dubo… Dubon… Dubonnet'.[15]

Savignac recommends beginning with the text, echoing Cassandre, 'Set it as far as possible in the centre of the composition'.[16]

Bernhard would be adamant. What comes first is the product. He invented the term the 'Sachplakat' or object poster. Show the product and the brand name. That's it – but do it with assurance and style (and no decoration) making sure that the brand name is not simply a caption. Note how Bernhard integrates the elements by making the matches a graphic

148

An Anglo-French pun which kept bubbling for a decade, even in Switzerland. Manuela Riva, Perrier, Switzerland, 1990, Agency: Marsden Lacher Studer AG.

Conversely, where real French is spoken, the pun is visual. Perrier, Belgium, 1993, Agency: Publicis.

Two puns. Perrier, UK, 1988, Agency: Leo Burnett.

YOUR TALK
MAY KILL YOUR COMRADES

A. GAMES.

Abram Games was a photographer's son yet photography hardly ever appears in his work. During World War II he was an official war artist. This, of all his work, is the design he was most proud of. Games, War Office, UK, 1942.

underlining of the name Priester (and is there just a hint of candles aflame in the lettering?) and by having the shoe overlap the name Stiller. The stark simplicity and fusion mean that in Bernhard's work motif and text probably impact on the viewer simultaneously.

Julius Gipkens, likewise, integrates product, name and descriptor by means of a fiery background. Hans Erdt (who, with Gipkens, worked for the same printer as Bernhard) associates the serious motorist with the name Opel. The capital letter suggests a tyre or maybe a driving wheel.

A contemporary, KG Richter links a tyre with its brand name Calmon interlocking the two circles. A Thirties American ad for Goodyear has the tyre encircle the globe. Julius Klinger, another Bernhard contemporary,

felicitously unites image and brand name so that the latter, rather than captioning the picture, plays a part in it.

Carlu makes a visual pun in his 1941 board for the US Office for Emergency Management – a wrench and a nut which is the O in production.

Note how Cassandre organizes the elements in the Triplex design, how the whole is held together by the inverted T (echoing the capitalized T of the brand) of the centre of the driving wheel which leads to the word Triplex.

An Instants lottery scratch card poster fuses the product with the lucky winner showing him in the act of being scratched from humdrum existence to a holiday situation.

The famous Forties Cola-Cola poster from a painting by Haddon H

Sundblom may seem unremarkable until you contemplate the composition: the alignment of the man's hand holding the bottle, the eyes of the girl in the swimsuit and that one word 'Yes'; the sweep from the head via the body to the red circle of the brand. And note how the girl's feet seem to be playing with the circle as if it is a beach ball. Remove any one element (as Milton Glaser says) or shift it somewhere else and the effect is lost.

But in this discussion on emphasis we need to distinguish between which is more important in the design, text or image, and the order in which the designer tackles the problem. Whereas there seems to be general agreement that the image is the more important, since that is what works first on the viewer, and that the designer's skills in handling colour and

pattern to attract attention are paramount, there is no consensus concerning the process of creation.

Milton Glaser says the process is not rational and that 'it is possible to describe everything except what is central'.[17]

I'll have a go, Milt. The brief was for a design for National Savings. The brand was the recently introduced Premium Bond, an investment-cum-lottery. What isn't won in prize money goes to the Treasury. Question: how to associate 'bet' with 'state'? 'Bet' led to 'flutter'. That suggested 'flag'… the Union Jack, big… the pole held by a figure, disproportionately small… and the line 'Have a flutter in the national interest'.

But in my experience it is rarely that linear. We could fudge this whole

Haddon H Sundblom, Coca-Cola, USA, 1946.

Driving wheel? Tyre? Whatever, the use of the O is capital. And it's echoed in the driver's goggles. A 'sach plakat' by Hans Rudi Erdt. Opel, Germany, 1911.

French poster artist Jean Carlu was in New York when France surrendered. The Office of War Information commissioned a poster from him to boost the war effort. USA, 1942.

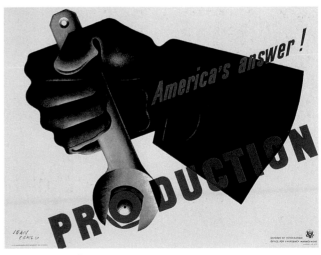

issue and say that the idea comes first – but that is more wish (or rationalization) than reality. Where does the designer dig? Into the brief I would suggest, taking out key thoughts, visualizing them. He or she might then take a word (Glaser invariably does), the brand name perhaps, or a combination of letters, or a word and a picture, mix, match, rearrange in the search for a new connection, an insight.

To repeat Paul Rand, 'The designer's role is to restate his problem in terms of ideas, pictures, forms and shapes… (he) extracts from his material by association and analogy.'[18] Abram Games agreed. 'Originality is secured by organizing known factors in new ways. Superficial technique is not enough. The basis of the problem must be discovered by analysis and reasoning.'[19] Others would not worry at it so much, pausing after initial study to indulge in what Jan Morris calls 'productive indolence', to let the subconscious have a go.[20] Or chance take a hand – as with the serendipitous 'Dubo…' Mark Twain declared that accident is 'the greatest of all inventors'.[21] However, as Pasteur said, 'chance favours the prepared mind'.[22]

The designer attempts to see things in a new way. He or she may start with the familiar and make it strange. As Alan Fletcher says 'What distinguishes designer sheep from designer goats is the ability to stroke a cliché until it purrs like a metaphor.'[23]

But the designer has to do more than see things in a new way. He must have the mastery of his art and the skill to transmit his insight to the viewer.

152 *A simple image of the product plus its name. Lucian Bernhard, Priester, Germany, 1906.*

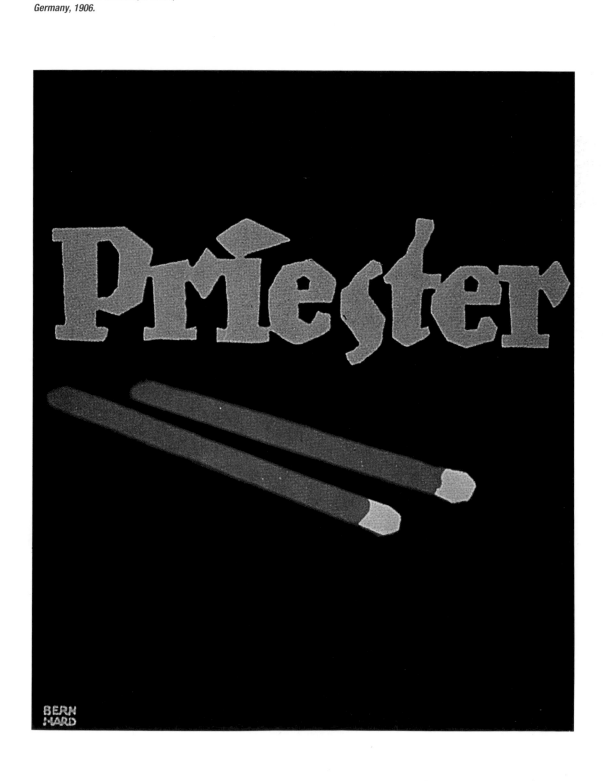

See it this way the designer says, maybe inverting the usual order of things. Kyösti Varis advertises a ski jump event by showing only the excited crowd. As early as 1908 Klinger chose to advertise an airport by depicting upturned faces. None of those magnificent new machines. But imagination can increase the wonder. 'Heard melodies are sweet, but those unheard are sweeter,' said Keats.[24]

Seeing it – and doing it – differently helps the design stand out. 'Get noticed. Nothing else matters', says Trevor Beattie.[25] Cappiello saw Thermogène as a pierrot. Another of his thematic posters was for Klaus chocolate. He drew a red horse. Customers would ask for Red Horse chocolate. A red horse stands out. I know of no pubs called the Brown Horse.

Maybe the start point is the competition. What are they doing? How can it be done differently? A naval commodore in a recent book on the Falklands writes that he based his strategy on his boxing coach at school, 'If they fight, box them; if they box, fight them'. Too often the competition adopts the same strategy and the consumer can't tell them apart.

In today's advertising agency pictures and words ostensibly start together. The team concept – art director and copywriter working together – is relatively recent. Some attribute its inception to Bill Bernbach. He and Paul Rand worked as a team on Ohrbachs, in the late Forties. It did not become the norm in the UK till the late Sixties.

The legendary poster artists, however, are lone individuals, their work

Where are the skiers? Kyösti Varis, ski event, Finland, 1973.

The alternative view. Kyösti Varis, ski event, Finland, 1985.

The artist chooses to ignore the newly invented aeroplane in favour of upturned faces. The spectators look like birds. Julius Klinger, Berlin Airport, Germany, 1908.

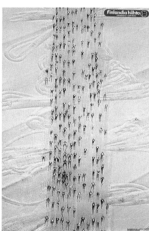

the result of a single personal vision. There are few examples of poster teams (The Beggarstaffs, Lewitt-Him). Today, comparatively few graphic designers are well known for their posters and fewer still agency artist-writer teams are known outside their own coterie.

When any creative team (from Bernbach and Rand to the youngest novitiates) hurl thoughts at each other the words and images are not in conflict. They are seeking synthesis.

We end this chapter with a quotation from an article written contemporaneously in Bill Bernbach's New York:

The function of the poster is, of course, to speak its message with the greatest possible impact in the least possible time. It must arrest, hold, persuade, implant an idea and give specific information. Pictorial elements may achieve the first ends, but text is almost always necessary for the latter. Thus, in judging the poster there are three considerations: how eloquently do the pictorial elements make their point; how efficiently does the text deliver the specific information; how well are these integrated to create a successful design entity?[26]

154

The artist's trademark was to associate a character with the brand. Leonetto Cappiello, Thermogène, France, 1909.

The character in this case was the red horse. It became the alternative brand name. Leonetto Cappiello, Chocolat Klaus, France, 1903.

CHOCOLAT KLAUS

DELECTA LE SUPRÊME DU GENRE CHOCOLAT **SUISSE**

Brand and consumer

We need now to return to the inexact science. It is easy to believe that the only advances in the business of advertising are semantic. A new or different word is introduced to describe a long-established principle or new terms are used to define and categorize consumers. An example of the first is *relationship marketing*. An example of the second is *super-consumer*.

Relationship marketing is built upon the belief that the task of advertising is not simply to sell a brand off the page or the hoarding in a series of discrete communications. Rather, it is the process of initiating and nurturing a relationship between the brand and the consumer.

This is hardly a new thought. As Judie Lannon writes, relationship marketing 'is based on the apparently startling insight that customers are more likely to stay loyal if the company treats them as individuals, demonstrates gratitude for their custom and does something extra'.[1]

'A brand', says the chief executive of Johnson & Johnson, 'is the capitalized value of the trust between a company and its customer'.[2] (Note the use of the singular. This is the age of one-to-one rather than mass communication.)

Marketers are being encouraged to think of consumers as 'lifetime consumers', to multiply the margin from one purchase by the number of lifetime purchases. And to add to that the possibility of sales of other brands which can be offered to that consumer from the company's range. With sophisticated technology it is not difficult to gain information regarding

158 *Mirrors in the underground for the beautiful people. Martini, 1996, Agency: Howell Henry Chaldecott Lury.*

lifestyle and preference and accordingly customize an offering.

Advertising is obviously not the only tool. Product information on and inside the packaging, personalized mailings, correspondence, company or brand magazines targeted at niche markets, tailor-made product offerings, consumer clubs, loyalty programmes, special 'privilege offers', face-to-face meetings, massive but not indiscriminate sampling … all are being used in this new era of one-to-one marketing.

A database can enable a company to pinpoint whom it regards as its most important consumers and keep up a relevant dialogue with them thereby encouraging loyalty and generating long-term sales.

None of these developments eliminates the need for advertising. Indeed, for some retailers advertising's role may not even change as the relationships are already established. Is it really too fanciful to see brands and consumers as friends? An urban landscape may be an intimidating place for a newcomer. A familiar brand sharing the street can be reassuring.

Each advertisement must be thought of as establishing and/or reinforcing a relationship. This necessitates understanding the personality of both the consumer and the brand. The brand must be thought of as a person with a collection of characteristics. These traits must remain constant. A brand should never act out of character. It can grow, add new features, spin-off a variant, but its essential character must remain recognizable and familiar. A brand which adopts a new persona sends out disturbing signals.

Volvo's consumer relationships cross countries. Volvo, Russia, 1996, Agency: Friedmann & Rose.

Volvo, UK, 1987, Agency: Abbott Mead Vickers.

159

Long before the terms 'brand image' and 'brand personality' became currency, some brands developed an identity by turning the product form or the pack into characters. Of these shown here, only the Michelin man remains. These designs are clever without promising a benefit. Lampo however, shows the vehicles it fuels.

Cappiello's Thermogène (page 154) is a personification of the brand, almost an organic growth. Most characters, however, are associations – e.g. Cassandre's Nicolas delivery man, Johnnie Walker or Aunt Jemima or satisfied users such as the Bisto Kids.

Atlas chooses to personify the problem rather than the brand.

Holsten Pils, UK, 1980s, Agency: GGT.

Atlas, UK, 1911.

The Michelin man was created by O'Galop, France, 1898.

Achille Mauzan, *Lampo, Italy, 1925.*

Delamere-Cerf, *Union Match,*
Belgium, 1926.

Leonetto Cappiello, *Fernet-Branca,*
Italy, 1911.

When Coca-Cola replaced its traditional flavour with a new one the damage, not simply to sales, but also to reputation, was immediate. When Persil introduced enzymes without announcing the fact consumers were baffled. In a focus group one of them refused to believe that 'my Persil could act like that!' What was being tested was the relationship, carefully built up over the years in consistent product performance and consumer communication. It was a relationship robust enough to survive that infidelity.

Marketers talk of brand loyalty. This is always taken to mean that the consumer should continue to be loyal to the brand. But brand loyalty is two-way. The brand must also be loyal to the consumer and, thus, to the heritage of the brand.

Advertising therefore, in this context, is not a short-term exercise. Specific ads will have specific tasks, some of them immediate, but the totality of the advertising is a form of continuous dialogue and reassurance. Manufacturers know that getting a new consumer is far more expensive than retaining an existing one. They assiduously assemble consumer names and details on databases. Technology will soon allow them to particularize their information to each consumer. A company with several brands can cross-reference information and offers. What drives this development for fast-moving packaged goods companies is the competition of retailers who have become expert marketers and who have the advantage of being much closer to the consumer. After all, the consumer actually walks into the retail brand.

This campaign was launched early in World War II. Persil, UK, 1950s, Agency: J Walter Thompson.

An early enamel for Persil, from a design by Kurt Heiligenstaedt. Persil, Germany, 1922.

Moreover, check-out technology and the smart card enable the retailer to know what each consumer purchases.

The first advertiser who realized that future sales depended upon consumer satisfaction and quality, repeated and guaranteed, was a relationship marketer. He or she may be somewhat more sophisticated today but then so is the consumer or the super-consumer as the fashionable phrase has it. Women are the dominant purchasers of fast-moving consumer goods (FMCG) and the real decision-makers in the purchase of consumer durables. As such, the female consumer is not the passive recipient of either product or message. She understands what marketers are up to. She is 'pro-active and demanding', asserts researcher Mary Goodyear, 'armed with product knowledge acquired from consumer interest groups … [she has] started to shop comparatively not only for price but for the absence of E numbers, the inclusion of vitamins, the avoidance of certain political incorrectness, etc.'[3] She is, in these circumstances, not blindly loyal but 'multi-faceted'. She may in fact change her identity as she changes mood, using different brands to express different parts of herself.

The scene is changing: though the difference is one of degree not kind. And perhaps the real change is not consumer attitude but a belated appreciation by the advertiser of the nature of the consumer and the complexity of the relationship between them. One consequence is clearly apparent – the consumer is keen to know more about the company behind

Old but new, just like the brand, the design echoes early posters in its use of flat colour. Annie Carlton, Persil, UK, early 1980s and 1988, Agency: J Walter Thompson.

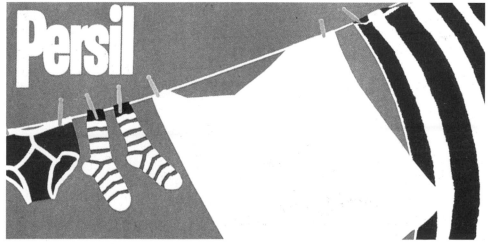

the brand. Environmental concerns have encouraged her to know, not simply what the brand will do for her, but also what's in it, who makes it and how they behave. Companies will not be able to hide behind their brands.

Against the foregoing, what is the role of outdoor advertising? An impossible question. There are different sorts of outdoor advertisements for different people at different times in different circumstances. What unites them are the constraints within which they have to work, the constraints which we examined in earlier chapters and to which we need to add the total factor of relationship and the part the advertisement plays in the *long-term dialogue*.

Most traditional – and much used – models of how advertising

works suffer from serious drawbacks.

They are *short term*. The process envisaged ends in a sale, rather than 'the creation of a customer'.

They are *one-way*. Whereas communication is an exchange.

They are *immobile*. They assume an unchanging consumer in a static environment, whereas the consumer's moods may fluctuate by the day, his or her purchasing pattern may be promiscuous and circumstances may vary.

They are *linear*. They presume a straight-line progression from stimulus to response, whereas reality is much less neat, more circular than straight. The classic model is AIDA: the ad is meant to attract *attention*, arouse *interest*, provoke *desire* and stimulate *action* (i.e. purchase). There are other

164 *Did this idea upset the traditional billposter? Seabrook, USA, 1989, Agency: Thompson & Co.* *Provocative inversion of 'Just Do It'. Nike, UK, 1996, Agency: Simons, Palmer, Clemmow & Johnson.*

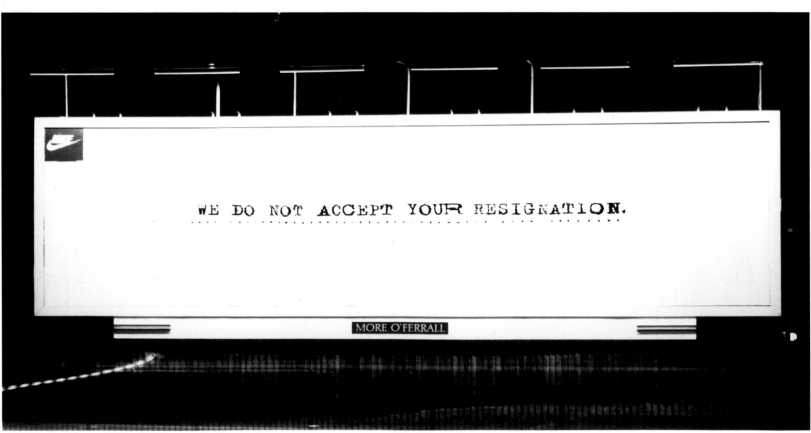

variants, e.g. awareness, understanding, belief, action.

Most of these models can be grouped under *sales response* (ad creates sales) or *persuasion* (behaviour changes attitude). There is a third category, what researchers Hall and Maclay call *the salience model* (advertising differentiates the product, makes it stand out). Much contemporary advertising is planned and created on this premise. 'Get noticed.' 'Make the brand famous.' 'Do it differently.' Nevertheless, this too is founded on a somewhat simplistic straight-line connection between cause and effect.

And though it is reassuring to advertising people when the case is proved, and sales are linked exclusively to their efforts, merely displaying an injunction is rarely rewarded with a transaction.

Print and TV advertising will allow an advertiser to augment the injunction with argument and association. But the limitations of the outdoor medium will presumably force the advertiser to reduce the message to an imprecation to buy. Many outdoor ads are simple commands. 'Time To Go To Seabrook', 'Pull On A Pair', 'Huggamuggamax', 'Taste The Right Ones', 'Lap It Up', 'Shop In Your Pyjamas', 'Kick A Little Asphalt', 'Just Do It', 'Indulge Yourself', 'Just Rise Above It', 'Drive Straight To Spain', 'Pick Up The Tab For Lunch', 'Keep A Cool Head', 'Get On A Roll', 'Unwind'.

But the interesting thing about many of the above commands is that they are not what they seem – they are not simplistic injunctions to purchase. Instead they are puns or their meaning is not immediately apparent. Today's

The can is the hero in a long-running campaign. Campbells Soup, Canada, 1989, Agency: Ogilvy & Mather.

*Outdoor Advertising Association
of Australia, 1994,
Agency: McCann-Erickson.*

The outdoor industry is keen to demonstrate its success in creating awareness.

In the UK the picture of a little girl appeared on sites throughout the country. Her name, said the text, was Amy and she liked snails.

After six weeks Amy's name and liking were recalled by 36 per cent of the population.

Another girl, Shirley Cothran, in late 1974, was crowned Miss America. She appeared on network TV, in magazines and newspapers. But how many people knew her name? Just 1.6 per cent according to research conducted in November and December 1974 in forty-four metropolitan areas.

In January and February 10,000 hoardings appeared carrying her picture and the line: 'Shirley Cothran Miss America 1975'. By March 16.3 per cent of the US population could tell you her name.

In Brisbane, Australia, General Outdoor Advertising invented a beer, Haka – a fictitious brew with a fictitious New Zealand origin. The slogan: 'Naturally Booed in Australia'. After four weeks of outdoor advertising, a sample of 300 eighteen year olds of both sexes were shown a picture of the billboard with the name concealed. 45 per cent recalled seeing it and three-quarters of those could correctly name the brand.

Then fiction turned into fact and Kelly's brewery obtained a licensing arrangement to brew and distribute the beer.

In France, outdoor contractor Avenir ran a billboard featuring an attractive bikini-clad lady who promised to remove the top on 2 September. On which date she promised to remove the bottom two days later. On 4 September the lady and Avenir kept their promise.

Naturally booed in Australia.

Avenir Publicité, France, 1981,
Agency: CLM BBDO.

consumer is hardly likely to buy a brand simply because he or she has been told to. Communication has to be more subtle, indirect and involving.

Moreover, command is only one form of sentence. (Illustrated below are the five forms – Statement, Question, Exclamation, Wish and Command.) Besides, even in an outdoor ad, taking action may not be the response required from the passer-by. At least not immediately.

Advertising is the communication of ideas about brands which move people towards purchase. Towards purchase. The path may be long. And where the consumer is on the path will determine the required response.

Stephen King envisages a 'framework for thinking how different sets of advertisements might work'.[4] The purpose of the communication may be to reinforce an attitude or modify an attitude. Or to bring something to the top of the consumer's mind so that previous satisfactions are recalled. Or to encourage the consumer to seek information. Or, finally, to take action – now.

Hall and Maclay identify a further model, more in keeping with current thinking, *the involvement model*. The purpose of advertising is to 'build a relationship with consumers by talking to them intelligently and entertainingly'.

Communicating begins, as we saw, at the end. And the word 'end' has two meanings – finish and purpose.

The transmitter has to think like the receiver, has to put him/herself in the receiver position before a transmission begins. No relationship can be

168 Statement *Pirelli, UK, 1995,*
Agency: Young & Rubicam.

Question *Coca-Cola, UK, 1994,*
Agency: McCann-Erickson.

Exclamation *Enka, Switzerland,*
1989, Agency: Aebi, Suter, Gisler,
Studer/ BBDO.

satisfactorily nourished unless the brand can empathise with the consumer. And, obviously, no communication can be of use unless the advertiser and agency creative team can agree before pen is put to paper exactly what response is desired from the consumer. *What is the consumer meant to feel, or think, or believe, or do as a result of seeing this advertisement?*

To reverse the earlier exercise, study the advertisements in this chapter. What is the intended response to each? Note how different they are. Few are as knee-jerk as 'I must buy the brand'. And, while you are at it, attempt to define the personality of each brand. Some will be easier to define than others. Could this be because you as a consumer are familiar with the former, that you have established a relationship with the brands concerned?

Of the others you may know little or nothing, indeed, may not wish to know anything. As Winston Fletcher reminds us, 'most ads are of no interest to most people most of the time',[5] (and thank goodness selective perception operates even outdoors). Furthermore, though you may become involved in a brand's communication you may not wish to take it any further. As with human intercourse, all relationships start with involvement but all involvements (or one-night stands) don't lead to relationships, meaningful or otherwise.

The concept of relationship has two important implications. First, since it is long term, the brand will be addressing existing *users* rather than potential ones. Moreover, it could be argued that, given the personality of the brand,

Wish *McDonald's, Canada, 1980s, Agency: Cassette Communication Marketing.*

Command *A US gas utility recommends conservation during the energy crisis of the Seventies. USA, 1970.*

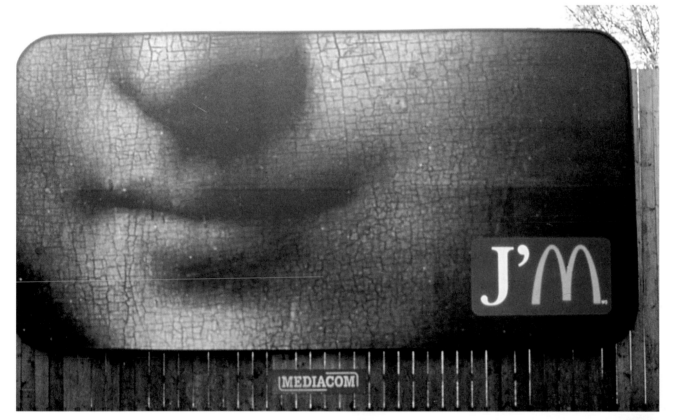

potential new users will be very like existing ones.

Familiarity, of course, may breed indifference. A repeated image or message or both may become invisible. The task of the advertiser is to refresh the known, but though the brand is revealing new facets, it has to remain coherent. Examine the campaigns for Guinness, *The Economist* and Volkswagen and see how the trick of being different yet the same is performed.

The brand must continue to delight the user in new ways – by being shown in new contexts or providing new services. Le Roy Merlin, a French household goods retailer, uses outdoor to invite customers to bring in samples of their garden mud ('we'll tell you what to plant') and tap water ('we'll tell you if you need to soften it').

The second implication of relationship is what one might call direction of travel. A relationship is two-way. The word may even remind you that communication comes from the Latin 'communicare', one meaning of which is to share. There is no communication unless there is a shared language, without which dialogue is impossible.

Relationship marketing in its latest guise allows the consumer to initiate dialogue, to do more than merely respond, for example, to access the Internet, the brand or company's Website.

But dialogue is no new kid on the block. 'Why does a woman look old sooner than a man?' asked Sunlight Soap in 1888. Questions famously

170 *Leroy Merlin, France, 1995, Agency: BDDP.*

Worthington, UK, 1996, Agency: WCRS.

Dialogue with a driver. Audi, UK, 1979, Agency: Bartle Bogle Hegarty.

adorned the walls in both world wars. 'Daddy what did you do in the Great War?' 'Is your journey really necessary?' A toothpaste in the Thirties asked 'Did you Maclean your teeth today?'(and the brand has recently reintroduced the line). 'Have you done anything worth a Worthington today?' 'What happened last night?' asks American radio station WDAF. 'Is this freedom?' asks Carrefour of manufacturer prices. The Audi challenges the driver of an implicitly ordinary car with one word 'Swop?' Coca-Cola asks 'Thirsty?' 'Got Milk?' asks a recent award-winning US campaign. 'What, too busy to call your mother?' asks Nynex. And Costa resorts to a simple question mark. An Italian funeral service involves the viewer in some fundamental questions. 'Why get there so fast?' 'How many did you smoke today?'

Dialogue can take place on the poster itself. And some brave advertisers have encouraged passers-by to respond to the poster on the poster. Some people don't need an invitation.

Posters have been known to speak to each other. 'Follow the leader', says the Honda bike. 'Don't follow anyone', replies Yamaha.

The famous Swedish campaign for Nescafé always features two people drinking the brand beneath the headline 'Nescafé!' 'Nescafé?' The conversation pre and post is filled in by the viewer. The whole exchange probably goes like this.

'This is good. What is it?'

'Nescafé!'

A nudge from the telephone company on a Manhattan sidewalk. And you can salve your conscience there and then. Nynex, USA, 1996, Agency: Korey Kay and Partners.

Costa, Chile, 1992.

Bizarre presentation of life and death questions from a funeral company. Eugenio Fabozzi, Onoranze Funebri, Italy, 1995.

Nescafé, Sweden, 1984, Agency: Liberg & Co.

171

'Nescafé?'
'Really.'
'I don't believe it. It tastes like freshly ground coffee.'
'This is the *new* Nescafé. Nescafé Lux.'
This ad manages to convey all that in a few words.

This is an example of both consequences of relationship – addressing existing users and two-way communication. The receiver participates in the construction of the message. This is not receiver as dumb recipient or target. The very word target betrays the one-way mentality of some marketers. You don't communicate with targets, you hit them – or try to.

Sometimes the dialogue stretches over a couple of weeks. Volkswagen show a vehicle almost entirely covered by a box and ask if we would buy a car simply because it was called Memphis. Later the box is removed and we are told that, apart from being a special, it is actually a Golf. The tone of voice is right: the relationship is reinforced.

Newcastle Brown Ale maintains its relationship with consumers even as they leave the boundaries of the city (see p 125). Nokia, who on Swedish streets ran teasers with questions such as 'Who makes the most toilet paper in Ireland?' (a question on every Swede's lips), also invited passers-by to solve puzzles. Nynex displays an intriguing illustration, a cow behind the billboard and the following week captions it 'Cow Hides', a listing in its Yellow Pages book.

Puzzle and solution.
Nynex Yellow Pages, USA, 1992,
Agency: Chiat/Day/Mojo.

A teasing question – but who is asking it?

Two weeks later the name is revealed but the puzzles continue. ('Draw this figure in one line without lifting the pencil.') Nokia, Sweden, 1988, Agency: Observa.

A medical insurance company for British and American expats in Poland displays the word 'Panic' and beneath demands 'Now Explain This In Polish' (see p 106). A week later a plaster covers the sign bearing the slogan, 'Relax. Join ABC Medicover.'

The advertiser can directly challenge the viewer. In a subway train a publisher reproduces part of a crime story and says, 'You have two stops to solve this murder.' On a taxi card a hospital asks the passenger if he or she would know what to do if a colleague collapsed with a heart attack (see p 185).

Many more outdoor ads, though not overtly so, are in fact puzzles. They demand decoding by the viewer. Look at Altoids ('Practice on ordinary mints'), the McDonald fuel gauge and Alcatraz's claim ('the original Hard Rock Cafe') ... the time between bafflement and elucidation, though short, is enough to get the passer-by involved.

Cigarette manufacturers have a long history of enigmatic advertising (see p 77) where the only words are a health warning. However, a hundred years ago Delft Salad Oil – the one with the two cart horses – featured a medieval tableau of battlement and maidens, a knight in armour and a dog. The puzzle is, where is the brand? Answer: bottom left, smashed. A Red Crown gasoline poster showed a driver looking puzzled. 'There used to be a hill here.' For America in 1940 that was brave. More recently in the USA the Honda car claimed it was 'the reason gas stations sell food'. A *National Enquirer* may come back as the *Wall Street Journal*. A US flag carries only

Altoids Mints, USA, 1996, Agency: Leo Burnett.

McDonalds, Australia, 1980s, Agency: Leo Burnett.

Double-take invitation from the tourist attraction. Alcatraz, USA, 1991, Agency: Goldberg Moser O'Neil.

Narrative painting. J Zon, Delft Salad Oil, The Netherlands, c1900. **173**

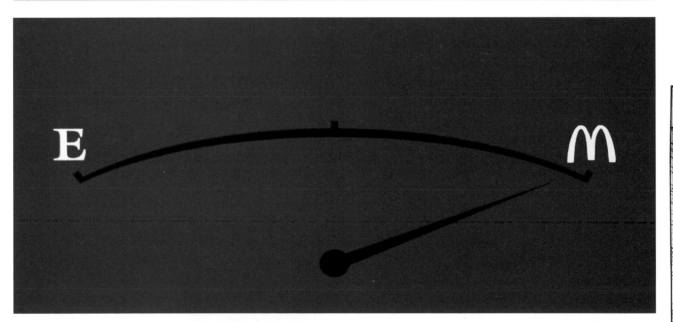

one star. Toblerone omits its fourth letter to say Christmas.

In the Seventies a Canadian radio station initiated a relationship with the passing driver by saying, 'If you're old enough to drive we've got news for you'. The mature (i.e. over seventeen) motorist catches on that this is a news station. The logo CFRB occupies the majority of the board and a line bisects it to indicate the station's location on the dial.

In Holland the Rover communicates its British origin by employing phonetic English to ensure correct pronunciation. In Norway an Esso station displays a chamber pot, and a fashion garment has a ludicrously low price tag (then you realize it's for the Salvation Army).

Humour is a component of many outdoor ads. 'The poster', said Savignac, 'is the jest that replaces a lengthy discourse.'[6] The joke is a good model of the communication process. It takes two to make a joke. There is in fact no joke unless the receiver completes the communication gap, until he or she 'gets' it.

The good humorous poster promotes that thinking feeling. A joke that has to be explained is no joke. There must always be a gap for the receiver to close. The size of the gap is critical – rather like that in a spark plug. Too wide or too narrow and there is no spark.

Humour allows the advertiser to say things via the receiver which if he or she were to say directly might not be accepted. Look at *The Economist* ad. 'I never read The Economist. Management trainee. Aged 42.' The proposition,

Involving claim. Honda Civic, USA, 1995, Agency: RP Alpha Group.

Recycle, Minneapolis, USA, 1989, Agency: Clarity Coverdale Reuff.

Delta, UK, 1994, Agency: Abbott Mead Vickers.

A lesson in English pronunciation for the future owner. Rover, The Netherlands, 1995, Agency: HGFV.

Much information, superbly targetted. CFRB radio station, Canada, 1970s.

proposition, of which this is the idea, is something like 'The Economist will help business executives succeed in management.' To put that in a slogan (e.g. 'Get Promoted – Read The Economist') would court derision.

The puzzle must contain its own elucidation. 'The best posters and the best symbols', says Kyösti Varis, 'both have a visual solution that offers the viewer the joy of sudden understanding.'[7]

The streets are alive with question and answer. Sometimes the words ask a question and the image answers it. Sometimes the image asks a question and the words answer it. Ideally the words and image ask a question and the passer-by answers it.

But that must not be the end of the exchange. *The Economist* self-evidently is maintaining a dialogue, developing the relationship. 'Sudden understanding' builds on previous understanding. Unless the promise and personality of the brand are being reinforced by the message and tone of voice, the witty outdoor ad is no more than a comic postcard or a motto in a cracker.

In character. The Economist*, UK,*
1993, Agency: Abbott Mead Vickers.

Need it say more? Esso, Norway,
1991, Agency: McCann-Erickson.

Get it? Toblerone, Canada, 1980s.

Beyond the billboard

Advertising people have a tendency to regard outdoor as one monolithic medium. Outdoor is outdoor is outdoor. It is, of course, neither one medium nor exclusively outdoor (the American term 'out-of-home' is inclusive). Print is not regarded that way. Magazines are different from newspapers, and no two magazines or newspapers are identical. Outdoor would not be so categorized were it the prime medium, attracting a larger share of the advertiser's budget. Being viewed merely as a support, the outdoor task is usually seen in simplistic terms, e.g. 'we'll reinforce the campaign with some high visibility of the brand message in areas of heavy traffic'.

Arguably, the most creative use of the medium is a result of lower overall advertising budgets with what would be regarded as a disproportionately (i.e. unfashionably) high percentage of the expenditure on outdoor. It is for this reason that lesser known brands pick up prizes at awards festivals. As the adage has it – 'we don't have much money so we'd better be creative'.

Being creative comprises both idea and media planning – what to say and how; where to say it and over what period – and making the optimal, and often surprising, use of the potential of the form and location. To such an advertiser the supersite and the bus shelter are at best distant cousins. This chapter reviews the extended family, i.e. what exists beyond the traditional 'poster' site, the billboard on the roadside.

178 *The Eiffel Tower, Paris, illuminated.*
Citroën, France, 1925.

Cadbury's Wispa, UK, 1996, Agency:
TMD Carat.

Transport advertising 'A moving advertisement which also happens to carry passengers' – a typical reaction to the bus totally covered in a commercial display. Mobile advertisements, however, predate the modern poster. Placard men carrying signs on poles were common in Britain and France in the early nineteenth century. Later came sandwich boards, a term coined by Charles Dickens. The competition in poster advertising (pasted-up printed bills) plus the advertisement duty led to the solution of carrying commercial messages around the streets. Terry Nevett in his history, *Advertising in Britain*, quotes a contemporary account: 'One man had a pasteboard hat, three times as high as other hats, on which is written in great letters, "Boots at twelve shillings a pair – warranted".'[1]

In London and Paris displays were also drawn through the streets by horses. Lotteries were advertised on moving carriages until 1826. Chests the size of small houses would be entirely covered in bills, causing traffic jams. 'Cheapside', complained a letter writer to *The Times*, 'is nearly choked in consequence of the snail pace of these nuisances – a van – with a large globe on the top and a man blowing a trumpet beside the driver.'[2]

The vans were superseded mid-century by the advent of omnibus advertising. In Paris advertising on fiacres became a sophisticated exercise with costs varying according to position.

Look at the horse bus. Does it remind you of anything? The mass of logos in a concentrated area? Exactly, today's Formula One racing car.

Is Kensington Church Street a brand?
UK, c1910.

Rate card for Paris fiacres, late nineteenth century.

179

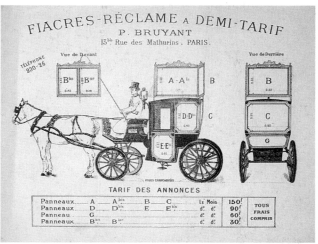

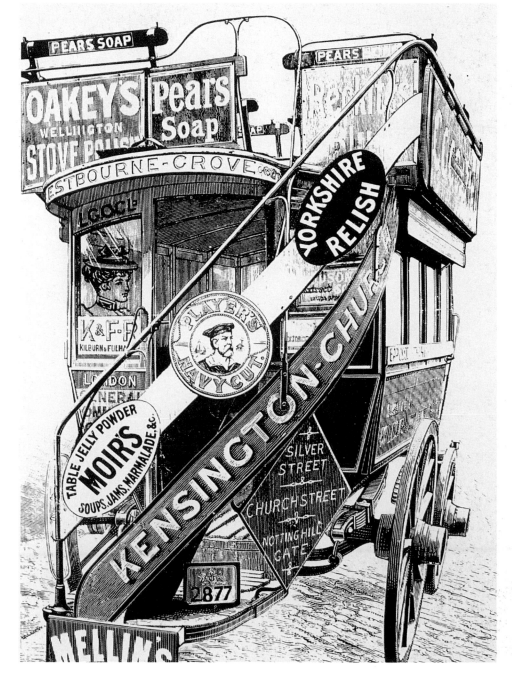

You know how it is. You wait so long for the sign of a bus and they all come at once ...

Moving experience

Missing People, Turkey, 1990.

Calvin Klein jeans, UK, 1995.

Novastrip, South Africa, 1989.
Agency: Saatchi & Saatchi,
Klerek & Barrett.

Big, striking and initially novel,
buses have become an attractive
option for advertisers. For some
they are particularly appropriate,
for example, addressing the
streetwise on the street. For others
they merely offer a large canvas.
A few choose to make a connection
between the capacity of the bus
and the message. Uniquely the
Turkish bus tells a sad story,
invites scrutiny and holds out hope.

Calvin Klein jeans, UK, 1995.

Helene Curtis, Salon Selectives, UK, 1996, Agency: Bartle Bogle Hegarty.

National Lottery Instants, Camelot, UK, 1996, Agency: Saatchi & Saatchi.

Carling Black Label, UK, 1995, Agency: WCRS.

Donna Karan, UK, 1996.

Plus ça change … External transport advertising, i.e. on the outside of vehicles – for pedestrians rather than passengers – allowed only simple messages. Almost inevitably there was room only for the brand name. The same applies to the racing car. However, whereas the advertiser on the horse bus was establishing his identity, his latterday equivalent is triggering other advertising and experience of the brand. As we have seen, outdoor advertising is all about movement. If he or she forgets that, an advertiser could be in trouble. You approach it, pass it, possibly pause to look at it, or look at it if you are required to pause… or it passes you. This essentially is a medium *en passant*. Unless you and the message are moving simultaneously which means, almost without exception, you are seated or standing inside the bus or train. Of course, you may be driving behind the bus and able to read the ad on the back. It is noticeable how many garages, car dealers and parts manufacturers choose this site.

External transport advertising provides even more of a challenge to the creative person than the poster or billboard. There is even less time to see it and the shape is usually unsuitable. There are few packs or products with the dimensions of a bus side. The temptation is to resort to words alone plus possibly a logo. But the difficulties are there to be overcome. A vitamin tablet ad shows a chewed pencil, some busy New Yorkers' idea of lunch. Some products are suitable for the shape – fashion items on supine models, rolls of confectionery, sausages, wine (the best are always laid down) – and

182 *Nike, USA, 1990s,*
Agency: TBWA Chiat/Day.

Lipton, Mongolia, 1994.

Fletcher Forbes Gill, Pirelli, UK, 1962.

ingenuity can often take care of the rest. See, for example, the classic solution of Fletcher Forbes Gill's design for Pirelli slippers. One ingenious advertising media man, frustrated by the restrictive narrow shape, suggested to London Transport that the centre panel of the bus side could also be used. Thus evolved the T shape poster which allows a standard portrait shape picture attached to a headline. Bus roofs have been utilized. 'Hello to all our readers in high office' exclaimed *The Economist*.

But why stop there? Why not take over the whole bus? Technology now allows all of the bus, including the windows, to be painted. Transport companies raise money whilst losing their identity by selling the entire external use of the bus to an advertiser. The results are often garish but occasionally witty and relevant. A South African bus is used as a symbolic demonstration of a paint stripper ('Catch the fastest stripper in town'). An Australian water authority gives the illusion that the entire bus is full of water. There is an impression of water painted on the inside of the windows and a message to the effect that all it takes to fill the bus with water is ten dripping taps. A Turkish double-decker is covered in bunnies for Energizer batteries. A Turkish single-decker is covered in photographs of missing people – a real social service – with the contact names appended.

In parts of the world where standard media are either unavailable or less suitable, transport can provide a dominant presence, especially in a launch situation. In Mongolia, Unilever painted a Yellow Label Tea bus for its Lipton

Coca-Cola, UK, 1995, Agency: McCann-Erickson.

Close Up toothpaste, Mongolia, 1994.

Painted train, Ghana, 1995.

Sponsored station sign, Ghana, 1995.

brand and covered the whole of a train with Close Up logos. A hundred years earlier a company which was to become part of Unilever, Hudson's Soap, painted its name on a gas-filled balloon and subsequently used press advertising to promote the story.

Transport has always attracted advertisers, often because they owned the vehicle. Shell owned theirs. It is often forgotten that most of their classic posters were pasted on lorry sides. A delivery van – for example for Fox's mints – became a moving sign. And if the shape of the vehicle could approximate that of the product so much the better – a topper for a hat manufacturer, a vacuum cleaner on wheels for Electrolux.

London taxis are constantly repainted – pink for the *Financial Times* or red and white for KitKat. Very occasionally the venture is coherent with the message. The United Airlines campaign is based on the fact that the airline spans locations, continents apart. So when it takes a London black cab it paints half of it yellow.

The wise advertiser will reinforce the message by taking the site on the back of the tip-up seats inside the cab. Here is an opportunity for a long message, addressed to the sort of people who frequently take taxis. When British Airways was promoting the comfort of its VC10 (see 'Images and words') the agency media buyer bought taxi cards. The easy solution would have been to reproduce the billboard design and get on with something else. Instead they thought about the medium, the message, the likely passenger

184 *Philips Radio, UK, 1930s.*   *Fox's Glacier Mints delivery lorry, UK, 1924.*   *Electrolux delivery van, UK, 1920s.*

and their situation. The ad said 'Even if your feet can reach this sign you'll still be comfortable in the new VC10 seat ...' Recently a London radio station, News Direct, installed telephones in the back of cabs linked directly to the station.

There were posters in panels in the coaches of early railway trains in Britain, but only in second- and third-class compartments. A seated passenger has time to read or – when the idea of advertisements within horse buses was proposed in 1847 – to be, according to *Punch*, accosted. 'How will you like sitting for an hour opposite to a pleasant list of wonderful cures by some Professor's Ointment?' A captive audience indeed. Sensible advertisers soon realized you don't win custom by annoying or boring

passengers. In the USA, early railway car cards tried to entertain with pictures and stories often in rhyme. Sapolio featured cartoon characters, the 'folks of Spotless town'. Heinz showed a mature lady studying the contents of a cupboard:

I always knew my son Jim's wife
Had found some scheme or other:
For she can't cook to save her life:
And neither can her mother.
And yet she always serves the best.
No matter when she dines:
I wonder why I never guessed

Transatlantic taxi. Part of a coherent campaign uniting destinations. United Airlines, UK, 1994/95, Agency: Leo Burnett.

A conversation in a cab could save your life. Ad on the back of a tip-up seat in London taxi. St Bartholomew's Hospital, UK, late 1970s.

A tip-up seat with support material. Talking Pages, UK, 1994, Agency: BMP DDB Needham.

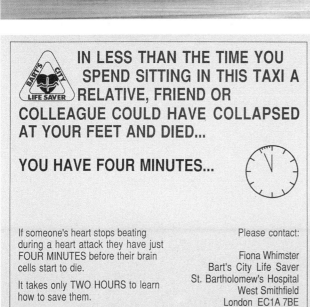

IN LESS THAN THE TIME YOU SPEND SITTING IN THIS TAXI A RELATIVE, FRIEND OR COLLEAGUE COULD HAVE COLLAPSED AT YOUR FEET AND DIED...

YOU HAVE FOUR MINUTES...

If someone's heart stops beating during a heart attack they have just FOUR MINUTES before their brain cells start to die.

It takes only TWO HOURS to learn how to save them.

It costs £1.50 - possibly less than this taxi ride...

Please contact:

Fiona Whimster
Bart's City Life Saver
St. Bartholomew's Hospital
West Smithfield
London EC1A 7BE

Tel: 01 606 3669

The credit's due to
HEINZ 57 VARIETIES
No doubt the rhythm of the train assisted that of the jingle. And, who knows, perhaps after three or four journeys, passengers were word perfect.

Even the faster subway train, with its shorter journey times, provides opportunities for encounters of the right kind, speaking to a consumer on a known route, indicating an outlet or branch next to an upcoming stop. There are even puzzles to solve. (In Singapore these are across track to occupy you while you await the train.) In London there are 'Poems on the Underground' by established and new poets. This encouraged Polo – the mint with the hole – to commission its own poems 'on the tube'. And if you're standing in a commuter crowd hanging on to a strap you look up and are addressed by a deodorant, 'Hands Down Those Not Using Mum'. In Budapest you are asked to raise you hand if you want a beer. In Beijing the strap you are hanging on to contains a life-size pack of the fruit juice which is advertised elsewhere in the carriage. In New York you can peruse a home-study ad and tear off a leaflet with more information and a coupon.

In 1945 the New York subway authority invited poster artists to contribute to a campaign to promote the medium in the medium. Note how the solutions of all three of the artists – Paul Rand, Sascha Maurer, Robert Orson – featured on p 188 are similar in concentrating on eyes and how different they are in message.

'Everybody who wants a beer raise your hands.' Borsodi, Hungary, 1996, Agency: Young & Rubicam.

Strategically placed next to the strap. Mum, UK, 1970s, Agency: Kay's.

Sails promotion in Bombay, to greet the arrival of the Prince of Wales, 1891, and Cowes, nineteenth century.

Actual fruit juice packs in hanging straps in Beijing subway, 1996.

A contemporary illustration of a late nineteenth-century London Underground train. Note the sponsored 'next-station' indicator.

Wherever there is transport there is an opportunity to advertise. Whether it's a bathing machine or the sail of a dinghy for John Bull or that of a dhow in Bombay Harbour when the Prince of Wales' ship sailed in. Or a plane skywriting Persil in the Thirties – or trailing a banner today over a beach. Or in the earliest underground trains in London which boasted an automatic station indicator 'sponsored' by Bovril. Or the whole of a dirigible, or the underside of an aeroplane. Or the wheels. A red London bus has white wheels shaped and embossed as Polo mints to introduce new Polo Strong in its red pack emblazoned on the side. While in Holland, Bavaria, a malt beer, replaces the wheel hubs with its crown cork. Or the billboard can itself move, via a trailer, cruise the streets and/or remain stationary at race tracks. Or a trailer can consist of a cooking stove with billowing smoke and the smell of Nanda's extra-hot Peri Peri Chicken. Which brings us to spectaculars.

Spectaculars Table Mountain in Cape Town, Niagara Falls and the white cliffs of Dover have one thing in common other than being landmarks. They have all narrowly escaped being used as the sites of giant billboards. The Dover site would have been visible in France.

In Paris, however, in 1925 the Eiffel Tower was illuminated down one side with the name Citroën. Today it could achieve the same effect with a deal more style by simply attaching its chevrons to the top. Ikea, the

Trailers are a relatively new medium in South Africa. This one with smoke bellowing from the car conveys a powerful message about Nando's Extra Hot Peri-Peri Chicken. 1996, Agency: TBWA Hunt Lascaris.

Bavaria alcohol-free beer on a bus wheel hub. The Netherlands, 1996.

Swedish furniture company, opened an out-of-town store south of London on an industrial site where all that remained of a power station were two towers. They were given permission to paint the tops with twin bands of yellow and blue. This is arguably the outdoor ad with the widest radius in Britain. Though perhaps more dramatic was the laser display beamed on to the dome of St Paul's cathedral for Cadbury. Battersea Power Station was another laser site. Irregularity of surface does not seem to matter. 'The image just wraps itself around', says the boss of the projection company. In 1996 Microsoft projected an image against the whole side of a massive building in Canary Wharf in London's Docklands and the year previously draped a Windows '95 banner from Toronto's CN tower.

Meanwhile, in Tottenham Court Road, tights manufacturer Pretty Polly has stood a supersite billboard on end to display a pair of branded legs. In Brussels an upturned board sports an actual Mitsubishi car to 'demonstrate' its stopping power; and a three-dimensional house is about to topple off a cliff (this for an insurance company). The famous Camel cigarette bulletin boards blew five-metre steam smoke rings in cities coast to coast. The giant A&P incandescent coffee cup in Times Square exuded real coffee aroma.

In South Africa real people climb an artificial mountain to advertise a radio station's coverage of an Everest expedition, a real workman dwarfed by the giant KitKat is apparently having a break and a real car zooms out of the billboard. In Australia two bridges 'bridge' the highway for United

Pretty Polly, UK, 1996, Agency: TBWA.

The car will stop in both languages. Mitsubishi, Belgium, 1995, Agency: Grey.

A powerful corner backlight in Santiago. Levi's, Chile, 1995, Agency: McCann-Erickson.

189

Airlines. In Zurich a dagger sticks out of a hoarding and 'blood' drips on to the pavement to advertise a play. A giant pair of trainers protrudes from the board for Reebok. A face changes strip by strip (as in kids' books) for Jubila soft drink. A car with its front crushed is elongated for a US auto bodyshop.

Moving displays are common. Drinks pour, cars accelerate, logos form, all sorts of celebrities make all sorts of gestures. And if the movement is as realistic as television, the words can be as up to the minute. Before the 1992 election, as the Conservative government's budget was announced by the Chancellor, an alternative budget was being displayed simultaneously on Spectacolour, the animated electronic screen in Piccadilly. The same site five years later announced the Conservative defeat. This sign uses ten

thousand light bulbs, half the number employed by the pioneering venture in Herald Square in 1910.

But there were moving posters long before that. In the last years of the nineteenth century on a screen above the Théâtre des Variétés in Paris were projected visual puns and advertisements.

I believe the grandiose age of the spectacular is passing. Size for its own sake may be a less attractive option when costs also increase and when planning restrictions bite. And does 3D add much beyond impact? The talented designer can achieve depth without it and suggest movement whereas the 3D board often gives the impression of a static tableau. In fact, there will always be locations where spectaculars are part of the scene –

190

Shower heads atop the site.
United Airlines, UK, 1996,
Agency: Young & Rubicam.

Piccadilly, London. Nike, UK, 1990s.

Times Square, New York, Camel,
USA, c1961.

The Brecht may be genuine even
if the blood isn't. Theatre poster,
Switzerland, 1987.

Los Angeles, Las Vegas, certain routes to airports, Times Square New York or Shinjuku in Tokyo. And there will always be new ideas – living plants, birdseed to attract real birds and the bus shelter in Johannesburg which was transformed into a gazebo! Ingenious and not necessarily expensive. A Dutch plant growth product Pokon chose to 'demonstrate' its effectiveness by having the actual poster site emerge day by day from the ground.

Street Furniture The term street furniture covers a variety of fixed items which dot the urban landscape, chiefly the sidewalk. Not all of them carry advertising though the majority of them are funded by it. Street furniture provides an amenity – shelter, comfort, convenience and information – to the pedestrian chiefly, but also the passenger and motorist. The contractor covers the cost of erecting and maintaining it, being funded in turn by the advertisers he or she attracts. There is clearly a community of interest between the contractor and the local authority. Both want the location to look good. Both require a pleasant and vibrant social environment. Leading architects and designers are commissioned, e.g. Norman Foster, Kenneth Grange, Richard Meier and Philippe Starke. The environment is improved for all concerned at no cost to the city or borough.

The business has flourished in the last decade in Western Europe, particularly in France and in the UK, the home of Adshel. It is flourishing, too, in the USA, especially the West Coast and New York. Environmental

Did the movie live up to the ad? Promotion by the film studio. Warner Brothers, USA, 1974.

Heralding spring, some major roads were graced with gazebos (bus shelters actually) complete with shrubs, fresh flowers and seedlings. Gro-Pak, South Africa, 1994, Agency: Wendy Dyer & Associates.

It's a growing medium. Pokon, Netherlands, 1995/96, Agency: HVR Advertising.

Solar-powered Singapore bus shelter. Malaysia, 1996.

pressures will inevitably speed its growth, as will the planning restrictions imposed upon larger highway structures. However, as we find continually in this study of ideas, the sponsored amenity is no new concept. We have already met the idea of a combined ad and information board in a subway train. (Indeed the advertiser was offering an amenity the moment he provided a calendar bearing his name or distributed a cut-out puzzle which featured his logo.) More directly relevant is the idea of sponsored seating, none so grand as the mosaic marble chair in Twenties' Tenerife advertising a Buick agency.

The makers of enamel signs no doubt found the sale of such a permanent fixture easier if it incorporated a service to the passer-by and,

especially, to the patron. The most common signs in France were thermometers. They existed in all sizes and for all sorts of products – chocolates, cigarette papers, face creams, mineral water, spirits, tisanes, soups, light bulbs – but rarely did the message connect with the temperature. A notable exception was La Vache qui Rit, 'Toujours fraiche même en ÉTÉ. Toujours faite à point même en HIVER.' In England Stephen's Inks's thermometer reassured the potential purchaser that the product was good 'for all temperatures' and Lyon's Tea claimed to be 'Degrees better'; the first claim being true but hardly relevant and the second relevant but not necessarily true. Sometimes the enamel sign provided a service for the shopkeeper. A chocolate laxative's thermometer also indicates the chemist's

192 *What's the suspension like? Marble chair sponsored by Buick dealer, Tenerife, 1920s.*

Denim seating at a bus stop. Levi's, UK, 1995, Agency: Bartle Bogle Hegarty.

'wares': 'Prescriptions. Drugs. Toilet Articles.'

Clocks came a distant second to thermometers. Today the positions are reversed, although both time and temperature are usually displayed digitally, together with local or commercial information.

Street furniture comprises bus shelters, kiosks, news stands, public lavatories, benches, street lights, clocks, freestanding panels, street lighting, road and traffic signs, and columns with integrated services. Contractors are careful to provide a range of designs – and to design from scratch – to ensure that location X does not resemble location Y and, more to the point, that, the furniture is suitable to the district. Specific services can be incorporated, for example, a phone in a bus shelter, a recycling point

for cans or batteries beneath a kiosk. Money-off coupons can be dispensed, or the brand advertised can be delivered from a machine. The freestanding sign can sport an ad on one side and local information (directional map, list of chemists and opening times, emergency numbers) on the other. Even the traditional Chinese wall newspaper has found itself encased within the glass panel of a freestanding Beijing sign.

The bus shelter can similarly incorporate information – not least, of course, about buses. Timetables – but more significantly an instant update of the progress of the next number 73 via satellite!

Sound units have been installed into bus shelters for Sci-Fi TV and Nintendo with a tape loop system. Following popular demand a digitally

Free-standing city information panel in Croydon. Colgate, UK, 1995, Agency: Young & Rubicam.

Immediate satisfaction. Ad-cum-dispenser. Mars, UK, 1996, Agency: DMB&B.

193

Martini Rossi, Belgium, c1962.

Belgian Toothpaste, c1935.

Cigarettes Boule Nationale, Warland, Brussels, c1936.

Benjamin Rabier, La Vache qui Rit, France, 1930s.

The first enamel signs appeared on the streets of Paris in 1847 – street names. The frailty of paper led advertisers to adopt metal plaques for commercial purposes, sometimes transferring poster designs *en bloc* but more often simplifying them further.

The durable medium endured till the Fifties.

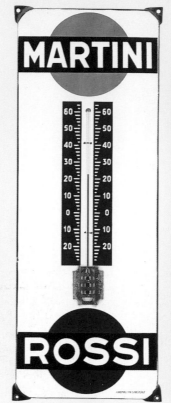

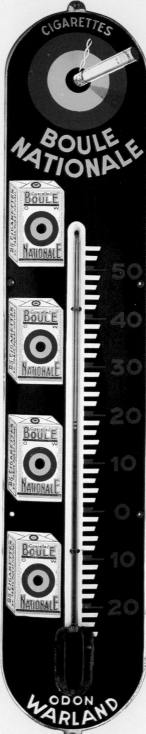

A beer plaque from the Fifties.
Enamels were nearing their end.
Sedan beer, France, c1950.

Chocmel/Kohler, Kohler SA, Vevey
(Switzerland), c1930, after a design
by Charles Kuhn.

Henry Weber, Tabac 24, Zurich, post-
1922, after a design by Luigi Taddei.

recorded micro-chip was developed in order to achieve a more reliable system. A cat, triggered by a remote sensor, purred from a shelter in Oxford Street accompanied by two posters for Spillers catfood Purrfect. Bus shelters have to survive vandalism (resilient new materials and twenty-four hour maintenance fight graffiti) and stand up to extremes of climate. In Singapore shelters incorporate cooling fans and water coolers.

In Britain Citylights, 1.8 x 1.2 metre backlit illuminated panels, represent the biggest area of outdoor growth. The reason is not simply the increasing number of panels available – either as individual signs or part of a bus shelter – but the expanding client base. John Scorah of Adshel detects a change of perception by the advertiser concerning the shelter's audience.[3]

Previously it had been assumed that the medium was best utilized for reaching mass audiences, albeit older and more down-market than the population as a whole. However, some 80 per cent of the medium's traffic is vehicular, passing the sites, not standing waiting for buses. This consequently provides an ABC, young audience and attracted greatest growth in 1995/6 from financial and fashion/cosmetics advertisers.

Traditional UK billboard advertisers – beer, cigarettes, government and cars – are somehow not suited to the size and proximity of the bus shelter. Younger audiences, not mass advertising's greatest fans, are more attracted. 'Towns would be bleaker without them.' So said a respondent in a qualitative research study amongst 15–24 year olds undertaken by Levi's.

196

Backlit bus shelter panel. DKNY, UK, 1996.

Three-dimensional backlit bus shelter. Pepsi-Cola, UK, 1996, Agency: Landor.

Calvin Klein jeans, UK, 1996.

Citylights were regarded as less corporate than their larger billboard cousins – and more intimate'.[4]

Street-level presence, backlit, illumination and a quality of printing the equal of colour magazines have enabled a few advertisers to gain additional impact and opportunities for PR. Technological advances have meant that a minimal number of sites, if imaginatively exploited, can leverage considerable publicity.

Guinness developed a back-printed poster for use around Saint Patrick's Day. A Guinness pint glass, empty during the day, appeared full at night when backlit. However, in 1912, London Underground displayed a poster of an empty theatre which, on becoming illuminated, filled with people.

Advertisers such as Levi's are beginning to cover all the glass panels of shelters with Contra VisionT which allows a one-way vision effect, thus not restricting the view from within the shelter. Levi's furnishing of the shelter with denim upholstered armchairs would no doubt have been appreciated by the patrons of the Miami Rescue Mission (see p 2). The sign on the shelter says 'House'. Beneath it the line 'When you're homeless you see the world differently.' 'We don't have much money so we'd better be creative.'

Technology Technology is being consumed by the outdoor medium like a starving man falling on a groaning board. Of course, not all of the experiments will succeed. Will fragrances – perfumes, soups, disinfectants

The glass is empty during the day but the structure is light-sensitive and the glass fills up at night. Guinness, UK, 1996, Agency: The Network.

Early technology created the same effect for London Underground in 1912, designed by Fred Taylor.

– pervade the air in just the right amount? Will speaking timetables annoy and frighten rather than inform and comfort? But the lenticular screen certainly provides depth imagery with an almost uncanny clarity. It can also be used to create flip images which change from one picture to another as the viewer passes the poster and sees the image from a different angle. Take this process one step further and you have animation with movement of up to twenty-eight different images produced on one poster. Although this process is still quite costly, the price is falling rapidly as it becomes more widely available.

Smirnoff has recently launched the UK's first campaign of 'virtual video' posters, with a large hairy spider crawling its way up a man's back.

If outdoor's holy grail is movement for some, for others it is change, the ability to replace one image with another. The first Multivision painted bulletin board was displayed in Sacramento in 1962. Triangular sections allowed three different designs to be shown on a single unit. But the mechanical nature of the system decreed that the changes occurred at set intervals throughout the day and night. Today the timing of the change and the length of exposure can be regulated by temperature or by remote control. The white sight screen behind the bowler's arm at cricket grounds can carry a message when the over finishes and the batsman faces towards the opposite screen. Why not use the same urban pavement site for a children's product during the day and an adult product in the evening?

198

Virtual reality. A crawling spider.
Smirnoff, UK, 1996,
Agency: Lowe Howard-Spink.

Railway station advertising
addresses a captive audience.
Marlboro, The Netherlands, 1996,
Agency: Leo Burnett.

Advertising for the film of Peter
Høeg's book Miss Smilla's feeling
for snow. Denmark, 1996.

Why not sell the medium like TV via 'dayparts'? Which is not the same as regarding it as a form of television. Flat screen technology can transform some poster sites into giant television screens such as Jumbotron (as at football grounds and at rock concerts) or Videowall.

New varieties of out-of-home media appear seemingly out of nowhere. Advertisers have forever put their names on carrier bags. Now they can publicize their wares on the tops of take-away food cartons or 'Adlids'. They are part of what is known as ambient media. Wherever people are – or, more importantly, *pause* – is a potential site. Fill up at a service station and the nozzle may invite you to buy a packet of confectionery or consider life insurance. The pioneering company, Alvern Norway, is active in sixteen countries. Its general manager bases the sales pitch on the captive audience and the proximity of the sales point. Even if you can't buy insurance at the station shop you can pick up a leaflet.

In a supermarket the trolley can carry a message – still or moving – and beneath the wheels you may find an ad placed by Eyes Down Media. 'Is there a floor in your marketing plan?' asks its trade ad.

Bamboo Lingerie used pavements for a new angle on underwear (see p 200). But kerbstone posters and stencilled sidewalks were popular in nineteenth-century London and New York.

Advertisers are taking tops of bus shelters, seen by passengers from the upper decks of buses. But signs on barn roofs were a common sight

Varieties of street furniture appearing across Europe. Tuborg, Denmark, 1996, Agency: McCann-Erickson

Europolitan, Sweden, 1996.

from the windows of nineteenth-century US passenger trains. And a typical line – 'Ayer's the old reliable Sarsaparilla is always on top' – reminds us that little is really new.

Advertising, for example by Red Bull energy drink on condom machines in pubs, or by BBC Worldwide videos on pub urinals may not have been an option for Victorian advertisers but introduced in 1874 into public house bars and luncheon rooms, were cabinets crowned by a clock and divided into advertising spaces each of one foot square.

Exactly fifty years earlier a patent was filed for a machine producing a twenty-four hour moving display constructed of wood panels, lanterns, lights and transparencies. The intensity of the light was adjusted according to the time of day and the density of fog. Today light-sensitive inks permit a change of message according to temperature.

Technology is a word derived from the Greek. The Greeks invented 'axones', a kinetic notice board which was placed where required. It listed for example a programme of sports events which rotated by means of a mechanical driver.

Today, when space is at a premium and ingenuity knows no bounds, when even police cars and street names can be sponsored and wheelchairs can carry the name of the local retailer providing the service, when technology makes short shrift of difficulty, who is to say where advertising may go 'beyond the billboard'? Let us hope that sanity rules.

200

New medium. New angle. Bamboo Lingerie, USA, 1992, Agency: Kirshenbaum & Bond.

Supermarket floor. Kellogg's, UK, 1996, Agency: J Walter Thompson.

Question. As you grasp the gasoline pump handle how many of the advertisers grasped the opportunity of your undivided attention? Various, UK, 1996.

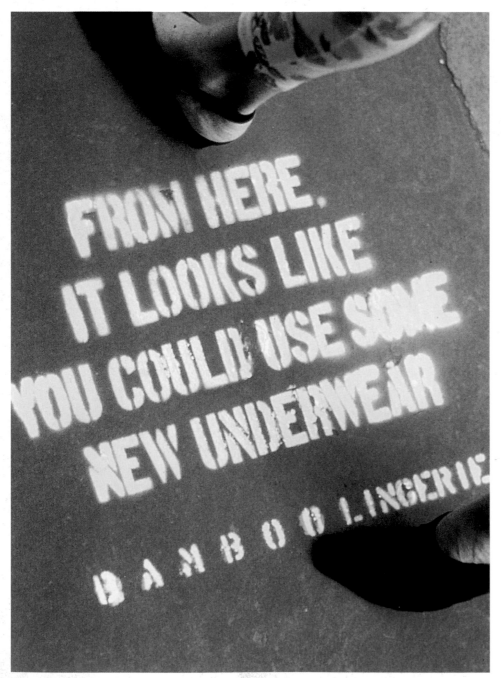

do you need **to be retuned?** pick up a leaflet inside for details
give me ⑤

Unleaded

Virgin RADIO
pump it up!
NATIONWIDE: 1215 & 1197-1260AM
LONDON & SOUTH EAST: 105.8FM

Diesel

tic tac FRESH MINT

THE MINT FOR YOUR CAR

Diesel

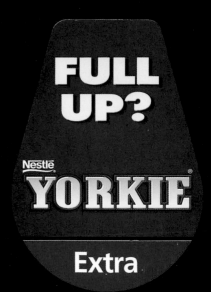

FULL UP?
Nestlé **YORKIE**

Extra

Tired?
CAUTION Do not drink when you want to sleep
Improves concentration
Red Bull STIMULATION
Improves reaction times
Improves endurance
Revitalizes mind and body

4 Star

YOU CAN'T HELP BUT PUMP THAT FRUIT!
ROWNTREE'S **FRUIT PASTILLES**
CONTAINS REAL FRUIT JUICES

Super PLUS Unleaded

HAVE YOU TRIED THE NEW MINT WITH THE HOLE?
POLO STRONG

Super PLUS Unleaded

NEW RED CARD EXTENDED ENERGY DRINK
KEEPS YOU GOING TILL YOU'RE SENT OFF

Premium Unleaded

SPECIAL MIXED
8 2
8 PACK ONLY £1·99

Super Unleaded

FILL UP ON ORANGE JUICE
Great Western Railways

4 Star

POCKET PACK
Cadbury's **DAIRY MILK**
Cadbury's **POCKET PACK**

Super

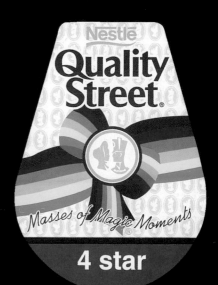

Nestlé **Quality Street**
Masses of Magic Moments

4 star

The future

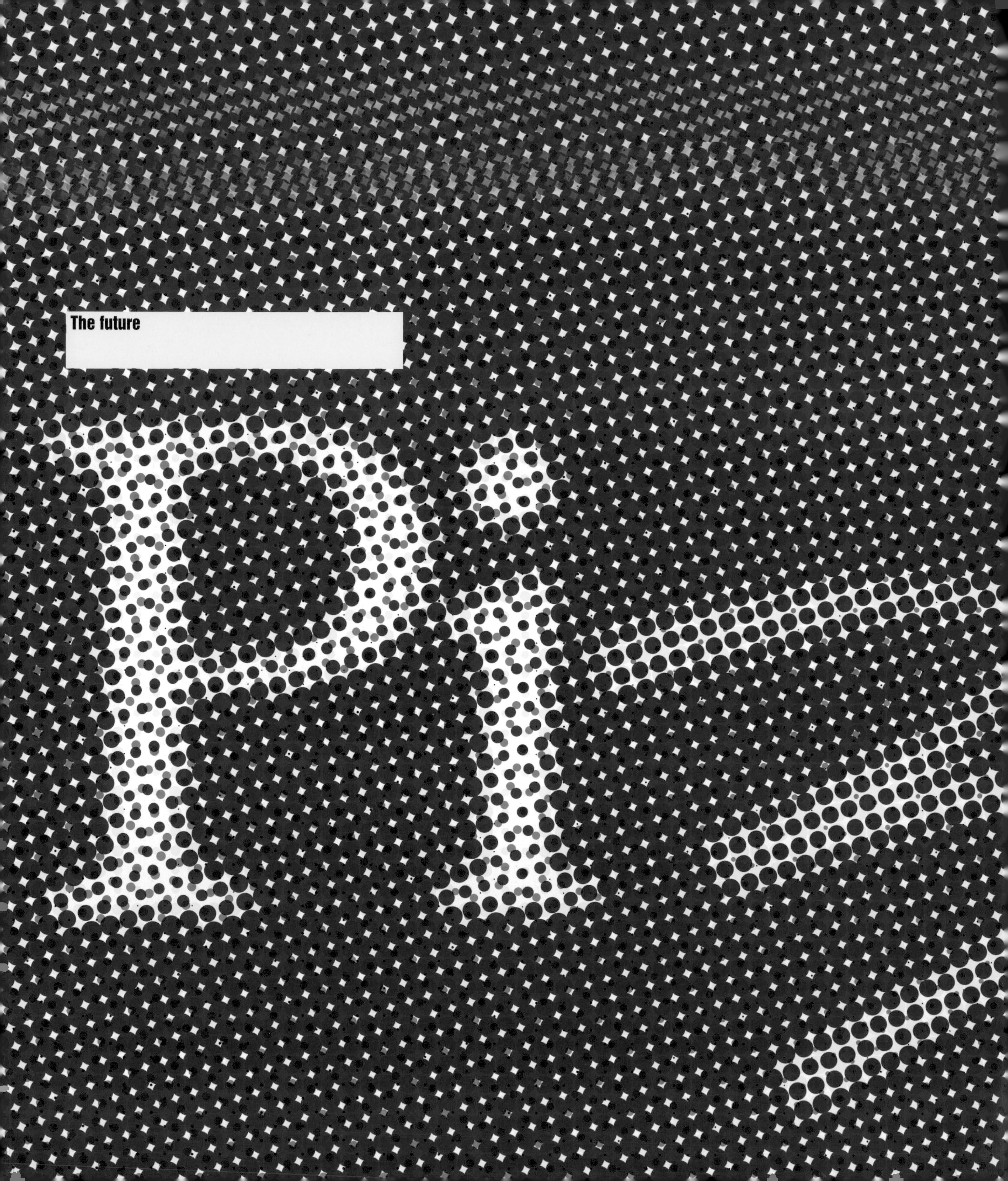

Twenty years ago graphic designer Heinz Edelman praised 'the unbroken vitality of this unruly grandchild of Gutenberg'.[1] The poster survives a century and a half after its modern incarnation. Chéret might not recognize it or be in sympathy with much of it. Nor is British artist David Gentleman in his *Guardian* tribute to one of the country's great poster artists:

> Abram Games's world has gone. People still design posters but no longer as a profession … Poster images are now mostly photographic. The kind of playful or surreal distortions, the visual tricks that Games played with paint, are now done routinely and anonymously on computers; it would not occur to anyone to wonder who had done them.[2]

All of which is sadly true. However, although the computer can routinely play tricks, is there a mind behind it informing the trickery – making the manner express a thought, cogently, concisely and with wit? Technology can illustrate an idea but not generate it. But Gentleman is right in noting the passing of an age. The integrated visual/verbal idea is rare today. Linkage between picture and words has largely replaced it. But some of us are optimistic, hopeful that the poster artist may soon be seated at the keyboard. Perhaps some already are.

The 'last true mass medium' is gaining market share in many European countries, is enjoying a modest boom in North America and is expanding in the Far East. Advertisers are returning to the medium. In the UK it is no longer regarded as the poor relation; or as the substitute medium because

204 *Adult advertising before and after the watershed. The Playboy Channel, UK, 1997, Agency: Maher Bird Associates.*

the advertiser isn't allowed on television; or as the medium dominated by a few advertisers (cigarettes, drinks and the Government). In 1991 35 per cent of the top two hundred advertisers were in outdoor, today the figure is nearer 80 per cent. Advertisers are experimenting with outdoor as the lead medium.

What is this telling us? Something of outdoor's importance in the business of advertising? Or about the innovation of the outdoor product? Or is the medium benefitting at the expense of other media – in a changing context? It's all of this and probably more.

In Canada segmentation of the TV audience – primarily because of the inroads of cable – has fuelled a gain in outdoor revenue, particularly in

consumer packaged goods. *Segmentation* involves selecting a medium to address a specific market – broad or narrow. But the audience has the opportunity of choosing from an increasing number of media. So we have *Fragmentation*. The channels multiply. The media scene shatters. The choices facing a media planner a decade ago were complex but nowhere near so chaotic as today. The jigsaw pieces of the Sixties and Seventies became a mosaic in the Eighties and a kaleidoscope today.

Advertisers seek 'niche markets', offering specific services and brand values to specific audiences, differentiating themselves from their competitors. The technology allows them to go further, to personalize their offering with massive databases and sophisticated software. The consumer

is no longer a fixed entity with a set of assorted preferences but a philanderer choosing among a repertoire of brands. The advertiser needs to know as much as possible about each consumer, and needs to establish a direct communication, maybe via the Internet. When the consumer logs on to the brand's Website all sorts of information can be provided, tailor-made to that consumer's life-style.

But in this different, exciting, one-to-one future two (related) questions arise. How to make the consumer aware of the Website in the first place? (Some advertisers are already using outdoor.) More importantly, what will motivate the consumer to access one brand rather than another?

While niche marketing and one-to-one targeting operate at the margin,

who is looking after the store, the core? As we move into the era of core-niche marketing (and, remember, you heard it here first) who is guarding the values of the brand and, as importantly, *articulating* them?

The guardian, of course, is the brand manager, with the assistance of the advertising agency. He or she has to determine the core values, approve their expression and find the channels along which they can be communicated. The outdoor medium could have a significant part to play in this exercise. Could outdoor represent *bedrock in an age of fragmentation?*

For many advertisers television was bedrock. It was the main expenditure in a media schedule and the central plank in the communication strategy. Aiding this was the fact that television was a shared experience.

206 *Changing faces in Osaka. Sharp Electronics, Japan, 1985.*

The Ministry of Sound started life as a club in south London. Its mission statement today is 'to become one of the most respected youth brands in the world'. Music, entertainment, merchandise, whatever. The brand

is all – rebellious and innovative. It projects its image on the Houses of Parliament, 1993. It hopes to do the same on Buckingham Palace.

The nuclear family sat around the set simultaneously with other nuclear families and the following morning discussed what they had seen. But life stopped being like that at least twenty years ago. Advertisers can ensure that the commercial is seen by a majority of the target audience but the cost is often exorbitant. Is this the most productive use of the budget? If they can communicate directly, develop the relationship, via other channels, then they may need to look elsewhere for a medium of 'shared experience'. Outdoor is seen by everybody. There the advertiser has a means of communicating a definitive statement about the brand, a public declaration simultaneously to a local, regional or national audience.

Or international. Outdoor is arguably the international corporate advertising medium. For those advertisers needing to be seen to be international, outdoor ads provide immediate evidence. They say 'we're here, we're important, we're part of the local scene, we offer the same values worldwide.' International outdoor campaigns are feasible but not easy for the advertiser to organize. Purchasing is complicated. There is no uniformity of size. Regulations similarly are not identical. But obstacles in the way of selling have a habit of disappearing.

Good works can also break barriers. In 1995 the poster industry ran an international competition on the theme 'Posters Against Violence'. The winning design was displayed in thirty-one countries on one day (See p 208).

The outdoor site is a solid and permanent physical presence. The

Posters against violence

Japan, Artist: Kazumasa Nagai, Designer: Nippon Design Center Inc.

Czech Republic, Designer: Thomas Machek, Design company: Academy of Design & Architecture.

UK, Designer: Alan Kitching, Design company: The Typography Workshop.

Switzerland, Designer: Rosmarie Tissi, Design company: Doermatt & Tissi.

Germany, Designer: Gunther Rambow, Design company: Rambow Van de Sand Graphik Design.

On 30 January 1995 a campaign was launched in thirty-one countries around the world. It had two objectives – to communicate that people could help end violence and to prove that the outdoor medium could be harnessed globally and simultaneously.

The audience was 1.2 billion. The message was carried on over 20,000 advertising structures – billboards, bus shelters, shopping mall posters and supersites.

The originators of the idea – Don Davidson, then of Mediacom Canada, and Edwin Yrausquin de Wit, media owner in Venezuela – enlisted the support of the Alliance Graphique Internationale, the leading design association. AGI targeted their membership and they in turn invited others to join them in a competition to be judged by an international jury (from North and South America, Europe and Japan). From over sixty entries the judges chose Mervyn Kurlansky, an Englishman working in Denmark.

Kurlansky's simple graphic tells the viewer that violence can be eliminated if he or she does something – i.e. pick up and apply the eraser. This was printed green in every country except the Americas where pink is the norm. Few other modifications were necessary. Six languages were used – Italian, Polish, Spanish, German, French and English.

'It was a remarkably gratifying experience for all involved in the programme to see the impact a single, simple involving poster could have on hundreds of millions of people around the world. It was the first global campaign in history – hopefully the first of many to come.' Don Davidson

The campaign achieved high reach scores (e.g. 85 per cent of all Canadians) and, together with supporting promotional activities, generated impressive media coverage. Virtually every newspaper and TV station in every market featured the campaign. Over seven hundred people contacted the Internet with their comments. Across three of the markets surveyed, the average audience level was 53 per cent among adults aged 25–54. Among women with children it reached 64 per cent.

These are figures to impress advertisers. But did the campaign reduce violence? That's a lot to ask and difficult to measure. However, the message that people have to get involved to reduce violence was clearly communicated – and civic authorities, police forces, schools and anti-violence groups got involved in the campaign. With many people it made an impression which will be difficult to erase.

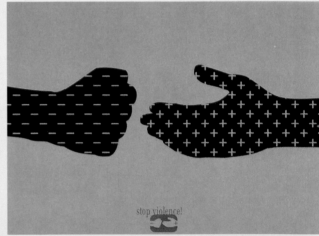

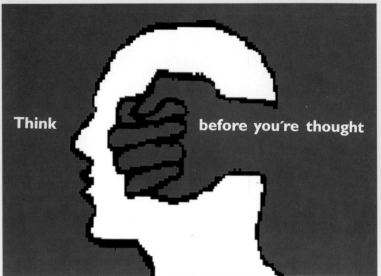

The Danish winning design on a site in Vienna. Designer: Mervyn Kurlansky.

message it carries shares those attributes. How many do justice to the opportunity? What would happen if advertisers were to regard outdoor as their lead medium? Would it result in more strategic and less tactical advertisements?

There is a need for a central defining statement of the brand to appear somewhere, a core around which all of a brand's communications can cohere. In the media turmoil there is a need for the still clear voice, for the message of a single mind from a vantage point above the bluster.

Whose single mind? The brand's – but also increasingly that of the manufacturer. With growing consumerist activity – especially regarding environmental matters – the company is stepping out from behind its brands and declaring its corporate values. There has been a significant shift in corporate advertising in the past decade. It is no longer the domain of 'prestige' communication to opinion leaders in the top people's newspaper or the financial press. In an age of increasing corporate *glasnost* companies are talking to a broad public – often from billboards. Colgate for example and the Belgian bank, BBL.

Why shouldn't a company use outdoor as a platform? Corporate was an early form of advertising. Company names preceded brand names. In China today corporate brands are significant on the outdoor scene.

Japanese and Korean companies – Toshiba, JVC, Ricoh, Daewoo, Hyundai, Samsung and the like – use outdoor to establish their presence,

210   *Hitachi, airports, 1980s.*   *Panasonic, airports, 1990s.*   *Corporate advertising on the Saigon River, Ho Chi Minh City, Vietnam, 1980s.*

awareness of brand name, prior to imparting information about the brand's products. Sony welcomes you to Singapore. Samsung have the same simple campaign in Europe, South East Asia and Moscow. And, where possible, trolleys in any airport. Between 1988 and 1989 ad revenue at London's Heathrow airport rose 60 per cent. One third of that originated from Japan and Korea.Hitachi also welcomes you to Singapore where Philips sponsors a sign: 'Keep Singapore Clean'. This is not so much product advertising but corporate public relations. As is their support of good art and design, following the lead set by Olivetti and Fiat in Italy.

'Japanese companies cannot succeed without establishing a cultural identity', says Kazumaja Nagia, writing about Shiseido. 'This means that companies must establish an image by contributing directly to society and culture'.[3] Though a company can use outdoor to register a change of name or, upon becoming privatized, to offer shares to the public, the chief purpose is to communicate implicitly its corporate personality.

An article in 1931 reported that Cassandre, 'believes the most effective advertising is that which, instead of picturing and talking about the product, impresses the spirit of the house producing it'.[4]

This is not to say that corporate and product ads are discrete. Every product ad is in a sense a corporate ad. Cassandre, who was guardian angel of the spirit of many companies, once described churches as ads for God and referred to Michelangelo as a maker of ads for heaven.

Corporate advertising addressed to the consumer. Mannesman, airports, 1990s.

An advertiser chooses outdoor to combat retailers' own brands. Colgate, UK, 1996, Agency: Young & Rubicam.

There is a related aspect of corporate communication. Here, first, is what respected London copywriter Tony Brignull has to say of the medium. 'No wonder posters are called the quintessence of advertising, the very Zen of it. No copy. No computerized film technology. No sound effects. Just one image and a few words to create a lasting message.'[5] And to create it immediately. There is neither room nor time for augmentation or development. The 'rules' therefore which these constraints impose upon poster creation provide the ideal mental discipline with which to tackle the task of corporate communication, whether the ultimate expression will appear on a billboard, in a press ad, dictate the commercial, or appear not externally but internally and provide the phrase which drives the company.

In the twenty-first century office – the reinvented workplace for a downsized staff on flexible hours at flexible spaces, 'hot-desking' with laptops and mobile phones – there is still need for the stationary, silent poster, if only to act as the banner to proclaim this brave new world. Chief executive Bob Ayling heralded British Airways' move to a new philosophy with posters declaring, 'Heroes don't have diaries'.[6]

The poster discipline could become a management tool as companies seek to sum up their core beliefs in a line whose style reflects their personality. And if that line can be communicated both internally and externally so much the more coherent.

The poster has been called the pictorial equivalent of a shout.

212 *Bottle of Hastings. Celebrating a previous successful conquest of the island. Stanley Penn, Guinness, UK, 1966, Agency: SH Benson.*

Benjamin Rabier, La Vache qui Rit, France, 1922.

Today we might replace shout with sound bite. ('Oxo – Beef In Brief' was a concentrated statement of the brand's benefit pre-World War One.) Today the outdoor ad is a SITE BITE, ideally an integration of image and message – simple but not simplistic.

With increasing media clutter and decreasing attention span, the outdoor medium seems uniquely placed to allow a company or brand to communicate what it represents pointedly, effectively – and repeatedly.

If outdoor, surprisingly to some, is the appropriate medium for the twenty-first century there could come about, if not a renaissance in 'poster art', then possibly a re-establishment of the role of the 'poster artist'. The tools, the means, may be different, but they will still be minimal and the meaning will still need to be maximum.

The medium's income growth will be determined, not by the volume the industry sells, but by the price it can charge for the increased value it can offer. In other words, there will be a limited inventory of higher quality. In the USA there is a shrinking supply of locations and an increasing number of regulations, e.g. zoning requirements and environmental restrictions. 'A farmer's field becomes a mall,' says US outdoor executive Bill Wardell, 'and four fine sites are lost.' Of course, the mall may permit a few smaller sites but the total space available will decrease. 'In Texas the authorities have decreed that if a hurricane hits and your board goes down it can't be re-erected.'[7]

Levi's 501, UK, 1993,
Agency: Bartle Bogle Hegarty.

Guinness, UK, 1974,
Agency: J Walter Thompson.

Jaguar, dealer sign in Canada, 1980s.

Audi, Brazil, 1990s.

VW Jetta, USA, 1994, Agency: Arnold,
Fortuna, Larna & Cabot.

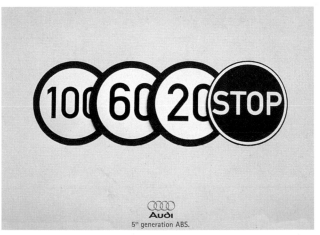

There will be a need for the medium to be more socially responsible. Posters are on show at all times of the day and night – and seen by people of all ages. 'There is no watershed', says Francis Goodwin of UK outdoor contractor Maiden, referring to the statutory requirement on television to restrict 'adult' expression till after 9 p.m. 'There is a duty of care.'[8]

The outdoor industry provides receptacles for litter, the collection of spent batteries, items for recycling but more needs to be done.

The opposition to visual pollution is growing. The future is with street furniture and new amenities (bicycle stores, gardens), not with bigger and bigger sites. There will be more barter between the contractor and the local authority – a win-win-win situation, a third participant being the consumer.

The industry depends to a large extent on the car. It has campaigned for road safety since the early days of motoring. Strategically placed displays have constantly informed motorists of ways to better driving. However, it could really practise enlightened self-interest by harnessing the talents of artists and writers, thus dramatically demonstrating that outdoor advertising works. Will it take up the challenge?

Contractors will improve their product, seek new advertisers, and new types of sites, entering into agreements with authorities seeking revenue, such as educational bodies. In Illinois, for example, outdoor contractors deal with a central committee representing 55,000 high schools. One is currently undertaking the installation and maintenance of soft drink machines and

214   *During the Euro '96 soccer tournament the Mars company sponsored this litter bin at Wembley Park underground station. The text is from a commentary at the end of the 1966 World Cup.*

Snickers, UK, 1996, Agency: Abbott Mead Vickers.

A Dutch local authority's dramatic attack on drink driving, 1996.

Airport trolleys carry not only luggage but duty-free purchases. Samsung, airports, 1990s.

internal signage. They will be produced at no cost to the state provided advertising can be incorporated. There is a 'duty of care' here, too, as commerce gets closer to education. (The largest provider of private pre-school education in the UK is the brewer Whitbread.)

What will attract new advertisers? Better evidence of effectiveness, of sales-related campaigns. Better research inspired by new technology such as that in the USA which counts the people who pass the poster site. Thanks to satellites advertisers can geo-code neighbourhoods via zip codes. They can, for example, take a 19–24-year-old audience and mark where they live, eat, go to the cinema, shop, go to the beach and then plot where they can be 'intercepted'.

The future, in short, will comprise new technology, new audiences, new products, new advertisers and new associates.

And a new type of consumer maybe – sceptical, advertising- and marketing-literate, regarding advertising as a game of cards in which the participants see each other's hand – in other words, postmodern. Examine the ads on p 215–17. Note the irony, humour and 'in-jokes', i.e. the self-referential consent. These elements are, according to Ian Forth of BMP DDB:

…often condemned by the modernist 'persuasion' school of advertisers of being self-indulgent. However, once it is understood that your advertising should nearly always be geared towards maintaining relationships with existing, or at worse, dormant, customers, these

A way to get noticed? Over my dead body. A press version of the campaign. Diesel Jeans, 1996, Sweden, Agency: Paradiset DDB Needham.

'Retro' advertising is a neat way of saying 'look at me' whilst actually saying something about the product. Nissan, UK, 1996, Agency: TBWA.

The approach is different so presumably is the soft drink. Irn Bru, UK, 1996, Agency: The Leith Agency.

Old-fashioned accessory. Old-fashioned location. An appropriate in-joke (inn-joke) for a brewery. Ruddles Best Bitter, UK, 1993, Agency: Marshalls Communication.

devices make dramatic sense. There is a private language and a set of shared references between friends, where strangers need to step cautiously around each other's sensibilities. A shared cultural background and a shared perspective on the brand's equity can often lead to advertising which is both playful and effective.[9]

Though postmodernism is primarily a phenomenon of the developed western/northern world the movement is rapidly spreading. As Forth points out, in South East Asia, 'the paradox of artistic mass production has resulted in an economy based on fakes'.[10]

People are not so much being manipulated as manipulating themselves. 'The astonishing thing is', according to Judie Lannon, 'that everyone knows this is happening and at the same time buys into it. People collude in the process as part of the price of an open, free-market society.'[11]

In the 'watching me, watching you' dialogue there is clearly a need for subtlety and fine tuning of communication. One advertiser will employ nostalgia because the brand has traditional values. Another will use an old-fashioned style of presentation because it feels that the viewer will share the joke, enjoy the parody. Or even, as in the case of high camp, empathize with the perpetrator's love of the original. However, the old-fashioned ad format may allow the brand to deliver some hard-hitting messages – so there is a double irony at work. Dash (see p 89) is a good example.

But the idea of advertising being *about* advertising is no new

One beer pays respect to another's famous campaign (see p 81). Heineken, UK, 1977, Agency: Lowe Howard-Spink.

A trainer distances itself (though not very far) from a provocative advertiser (see p 63). Nike, UK, 1994, Agency: Simons Palmer Denton Clemmow & Johnson.

You don't have to wait for a bus to go on a trip. Stimorol chewing gum, The Netherlands, 1997.

A mint shares a joke – and product values – with a mineral water (see p 148). Polo, UK, 1994, Agency: J Walter Thompson.

development for the outdoor medium. In early designs a simple means of incorporating the brand name was to feature a poster within it. Early designs for Rowntree's, Lux, Maggi (see p 47) featured posters or enamels: it was a convenient means of incorporating the brand name. Recently the Patrick agency in the USA produced a sales video which featured commercials which showed billboards – being erected, walked into, communicating with each other.

Self-referential, self-indulgent, schizoid, incestuous maybe – but at least the advertisement is not pretending to be something else!

Postmodernism, the academics tell us, decrees a levelling of distinction between mass culture and high culture. In the words of Feyerabend,

'anything goes'.[12] Art and commercial art merge in the outdoor ad. The wheel has come full circle.

Is the poster the place for the avant garde? Or indeed is advertising? Previously one would have said, 'No, advertising doesn't set trends, it follows them.' However, in a postmodern age with the consumer ad-literate and sceptical, advertisers have to be ahead. A young magazine editor recently alleged that any marketing executive who believed he or she understood the youth market was already out of touch. Furthermore, technological advances can be quickly caught up. So, as FMCG manufacturers realize what *fast-moving* really means, maybe there is a need for advertising to do things which are new, different and controversial.

'Imitation is the sincerest form of flattery', said Doctor Johnson. Advertisers, however, prefer to know in advance and co-operate in the process. Here are three examples of planned adjacent posters. A beer ties

in with a weekly magazine. A non-alcoholic beer promises performance. An outdoor contractor sells the actual type of site.

Carling, UK, 1996, Agency: WCRS.

Kaliber, UK, 1996, Agency: Euro RSCG Wneck Gosper.

Mills and Allen, UK, 1996.

Then of course there's unplanned adjacent posting … UK, 1940s.

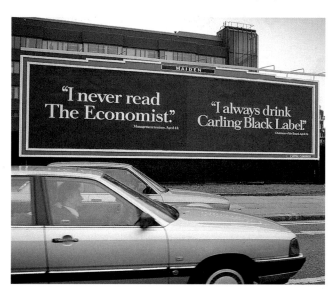

Here's another maverick prediction. As attention span decreases so commercials will shorten and become simpler. They will be made with one eye on the fast forward of the video recorder. They will become posters. (You can try this for yourself. Next time you view a programme you have recorded and fast forward through the commercial break check which ads stand out.)

There is one prediction which is less maverick, and less personal. It concerns outdoor's future role as the bedrock medium. Other people – from the industry and agencies – use other metaphors. The director of the UK's Outdoor Advertising Association says, 'Media fragmentation makes outdoor a more connective tissue for all campaigns.'[13]

His opposite number in the US refers to out-of-home as a compass.

'It represents magnetic north.'[14] A spokesman for a French contractor mixes a neat metaphor. 'Outdoor will become an umbrella medium, providing the glue that holds many other diverse niche media together in a consistent whole.'[15] A US agency man, blithely dismissing any fear of 'obsolescence in the face of existing and emerging electronic media', manages no fewer than three metaphors. 'It's like a little security blanket, planting your flag in front of the consumer. It's the yin to the other media's yang.'[16]

As this chapter I hope has shown, on many of the marketing and communication issues facing companies today – fragmentation, social responsibility, environment, global communication, limited attention span – the outdoor industry has something relevant and important to say.

218 *Four posters from a campaign which is unnecessarily more than honest. 'Reverse hyperbole'. Budget Hotel, The Netherlands, 1995.*

'Limited attention span? We've been in the limited attention span business for 150 years!' John Hegarty, creative director of BBH, has the penultimate word:

As we hurtle towards a world of over-choice, with increasingly little time to make those choices, the oldest advertising medium in the world becomes the most important. And as media fragmentation continues, so the poster becomes virtually the only medium that binds us together as one culture.[17]

But, astonishingly the word which best describes outdoor – both media and advertisement – is the one which we have used or maybe misused all along: *support*. Not in the sense of 'playing a subordinate part', but 'bearing the weight of'. Not a bit player but the platform.

Timely digital caption. Kilkenny, UK, 1996, Agency: Publicis.

219

Postscript

During the thirty years or so that the art of advertising has been fashionable a great many books on posters have been published. If all these studies have given due credit to the pioneers of advertising art, they have each, generally, chosen an historical approach, more applicable to art criticism than commerce; and the communicative aspect of advertising has largely remained undiscussed. Those publications focusing straightforwardly on advertising, on the other hand, have tended to content themselves with reproducing a selection of recent creations, without a reflective and critical text to accompany them. Uniquely, this book combines historical insight with contemporary critique.

Having read this examination of the many facets of the outdoor medium, you will have seen historical posters by all the incontestable past masters of the advertising art, alongside a collection of international contemporary work which is impressive in its variety and quality. In covering the whole recorded history of outdoor advertising, we can thereby follow the stylistic *and* the sociological evolution of the medium. It is in fact a record of innovatory solutions, period by period; thus, one can see clearly how, from Chéret to the present day, the role of the poster, and the conception of advertising, has altered.

David Bernstein's skill, however, lies in being able to distil the medium in a way that is both enlightening and unexpected. Thus in the chapter on 'Art and Advertising', for example, where one might expect a literal pictorial explanation, this is not given. One might feel outraged to find that in this section there is only a single poster by Cassandre – it must be an injustice, a mistake! But as one continues, each of Cassandre's principal works are then represented throughout the book, judiciously placed as examples in a larger discussion. Chapter after chapter, the juxtaposition of posters from different periods and countries cleverly illustrates a continuing line of argument which is that outdoor advertising is a medium whose principles and methods are enduring. Refined and honed over time by succeeding generations of poster artists and creative directors, they are focussed increasingly sharply on doing 'more with less'; on communicating effectively in the blinking of an eye, whether it be from a billboard, or the back of a bus. As David Bernstein has observed: 'To succeed in outdoor is to pass the supreme creative test'.

The vision presented here is truly international; the best examples are brought together in a global vision of advertising art. The confrontation of different styles is certainly educational, but can also be strongly diverting, notably in the small thematic niches, the playful interludes, with which David Bernstein has punctuated his text.

This book, therefore, presents a truly broad general survey, rich in thoughts, with examples and pictures which, thus assembled, make up a fresco that is as lively as it is passionate. I think that on reading this work, he will have convinced you – as he and I both are – of the vivacity of a medium which, even as one of the oldest in the world, can confidently approach the third millennium.

Alain Weill

Formerly curator of the Musée de l'Affiche, Paris

Poster Sizes

UK poster sizes are still referred to by the multiples of sheets used to make up the final size.

The basic sheet was the original 'Double Crown' (30 inches by 20 inches) which was the smallest size of poster in commercial use, i.e. by publishers in bookstalls in the 1920s and by other advertisers on the front and rear of buses.

A 16 sheet vertical poster is thus ten feet high (i.e. 4 times 30 inches) and 6 feet 8 inches wide (i.e. 4 times 20 inches) or approximately 3 metres by 2 metres.

Three of these side by side make up a 48 sheet horizontal poster – 3 metres by 6 metres. Bulletin boards and supersites are roughly the same. 64 sheets and 96 sheets are proportionately wider whilst retaining the same height.

Four sheets (1.5 metres by 1 metre) became popular with the emergence of Adshel and shopping precincts.

The USA also based formats on sheets, though of different sizes. The 30 sheet poster is 2.9 metres by 6.6 metres. The 8 sheet or 'junior panel' is 1.5 metres by 3.4 metres.

Bulletins are usually custom made in the USA and Canada. A common size is 4.3 metres by 14.6 metres.

Though proportions may be similar around the world there is no such thing as a standard international size. In the Far East for example there are structures 10 metres high and anything from 7 metres (Japan) to 24 and 30 metres (Thailand) and 36 metres (Philippines) wide.

A fairly common global size, however, is the 6 sheet, 2.3 metres by 1 metre.

The two most commonly used poster sizes for the same recent Levi's campaign. (Not for arachnaphobics!) The horizontal 48 sheet poster, Levi Strauss, UK, 1997, Agency: Bartle Bogle Hegarty.

The spider is even more intimidating in the vertical 16 sheet poster, Levi Strauss, UK, 1997, Agency: Bartle Bogle Hegarty.

Researching the outdoor medium

Sites by major junctions have the highest impact on passers-by. National Lottery, UK, 1997, Agency: Saatchi & Saatchi.

No creative execution is worth anything unless it is seen by the people to whom it is addressed (the target audience).

Having invested in creative development and, more heavily, in buying the space, the advertiser needs to know how efficient has been his expenditure in terms of audience delivery.

Evaluation must start with an assessment of the target audience's opportunity to see each separate advertisement (OTS) and an accumulation of this into a total OTS for the whole campaign.

Obviously, not everybody sees the same number of ads – indeed, some see none at all. It is therefore important to understand more about individual media consumption patterns to estimate how many people have seen one or more advertisements (cover or reach) and the average number of times they have had an opportunity to see the advertising (average OTS).

Outdoor has traditionally been the poor relation in audience measurement, the available figures regarded as inflated or unrealistic. The closest any country has come to satisfactory measurement of OTS in outdoor has been through the use of traffic counts (pedestrian and vehicular) at particular locations. As governments and local authorities collected more 'official' data, so more counts became available to the outdoor industry.

The United States (through their Traffic Audit Bureau), France and particularly the United Kingdom have led the way with this form of measurement. However, traffic past a particular location is not comparable with presence in the room with a TV set switched on or seeing the average issue of a newspaper, magazine or periodical as an acceptable measurement of an OTS.

This data took no account of individual poster characteristics such as deflection from the sight line or angle of viewing. In 1996 POSTAR was launched in the UK. POSTAR sets out to provide an estimate of OTS generated by the traffic past every poster site in the country.

– an estimate of those likely to receive an impact from the advertising on the panel and
– an estimate of the cover and frequency of any campaign.

In order to overcome the lack of actual traffic counts at every location POSTAR has taken advantage of a new technique called 'Neural Network' modelling. This is a semi-intelligent computer system which looks at actual data – in this case 10,000 local authority traffic counts, 9,000 pedestrian counts and individual site details and, by 'learning' the significance of certain characteristics, it makes a 'best estimate' of traffic at locations it knows nothing about. This Neural Network modelling has been validated to a high level of confidence.

These traffic estimates now provide the basis for estimating the OTS for each panel in the outdoor medium. These OTS needed to be modified to provide a better estimate of those likely to receive an impact from the advertising on the panel. This problem was tackled by means of an advance visibility study, conducted by the Department of Psychology at Birkbeck College, London University, to evaluate how people actually look at posters. In a highly ingenious study respondents, believing they were taking part in a road safety experiment, played one of three roles – driver, passenger or pedestrian – and were exposed to images of posters in various typical road situations. An eye camera, using infra-red technology, to measure eye movements, revealed what they actually looked at. The analysis of over 63,000 eye movement observations showed how visibility varies dependent on panel size, angle, distance from the kerbside, illumination, clutter and other factors. As a result, it was possible to devise a 'visibility factor' which, when applied to each panel OTS, produced a realistic estimate not just of those having the opportunity to see the panel but also those taking the opportunity and receiving an impact from the advertisement on the panel.

Arguably, this research has moved outdoor measurement ahead of other media. It equates to 'attention' to a commercial rather than presence in a room or reading the average page, rather than just the issue; information not generally published by the TV and Press media.

Finally this data for each site/panel needed to be accumulated and a method of estimating the reach and frequency of a poster campaign developed taking account of the duration of the campaign and the location of the component sites.

POSTAR instituted a Travel Survey which tracked over 80,000 actual journeys from a representative sample of 75,000 adults from 140 sampling points throughout the UK. Four hundred of these were revisited over a four-week period to ascertain travel patterns over time. The journeys were then mapped to establish passages past actual poster panels and the data collected was used as the basis for the reach and frequency models.

New technologies will change even further the ability to accurately predict OTS reach and frequency in the Outdoor medium. One example is the use of GPS (Satellite Geo Positioning System) and radio to get absolute fixes on journey patterns. A small transmitter can be worn by each individual in a sample and actual travel patterns logged. Using this technology would enhance significantly the reach and frequency data currently available providing a real fix on multiple OTS (by knowing how many times the individual passes the same panel) and even better determination of the number of panels required to deliver particular levels of reach.
Chris Dickens
Chairman of POSTAR

MIDWEEK DRAW, EVERY WEEK FROM FEBRUARY 5TH.
IT COULD BE YOU.
THE NATIONAL LOTTERY®
MORE O'FERRALL

Notes

Notes

Introduction
1. Andy Warhol, interview in TV documentary, *Painters Painting*, New York, 1972.

Art and advertising
1. Frank Presbrey, *The History and Development of Advertising*, Doubleday (New York), 1929.
2. Henry Nocq, *Tendances Nouvelles, Enquête sur l'évolution des industries d'art*, H Floury (Paris), 1896.
3. Charles Hiatt, *Picture Posters*, George Bell (London), 1895.
4. Dick Dooijes and Pieter Brattinga, *A History of the Netherlands Poster*, Scheltema & Holkema (Amsterdam), 1968.
5. Raymond Needham, article in *The Poster and Art Collector*, volume vi, April/May, 1901.
6. Clive Bell, *The Metaphysical Hypothesis*, in *Art*, 1914.
7. Hiatt, *op cit*.
8. Hiatt, *op cit*.
9. Abram Games, in conversation with the author.
10. Attilio Rossi, *I manifesti*, Fratelli Fabbri Editori, 1966. Translated by Raymond Rudorf, *Posters*, Hamlyn (London), 1969.
11. Daniel Boorstin, *The Creators – a history of heroes of the imagination*, Random House (New York), 1992.
12. Irma A Richter (ed), *Selections from the notebooks of Leonardo da Vinci*, World's Classics (Oxford), 1952.
13. Joseph Conrad, *The Nigger of the Narcissus* (preface), 1897.
14. Paul Valéry, quoted in Pierre Belvès, *Les yeux ouverts sur l'art*, Jeunesse 2000, Hachette (Paris), 1972.
15. Paul Klee, *Creative Credo*, 1918, quoted in Ian Crofton (ed), *A Dictionary of Art Quotations*, Routledge (London), 1988.
16. Leo Burnett, quoted in David Ogilvy, *Ogilvy on Advertising*, Pan Books (London), 1983.
17. Otto Treumann, quoted in interview with Anthon Beeke, *Affiche* magazine, no 5, Wabnitz Editions, Arnhem, March 1993.
18. Abram Games, *Pattern and Purpose*, a paper given at International Design Conference, Aspen, Colorado, June 1959.
19. Henri Mouron, *Cassandre – Affiches, Arts Graphiques, Theatre*, Skira, Geneva, 1985.
20. Foreword, *Expresionismus a ceskéuméní*, exhibition catalogue, Narodny Gallery (Prague), 1994.
21. *PM Weekly*, quoted by Christopher de Noon, *Posters of the WPA*, The Wheatley Press (Los Angeles), 1987.
22. Stephen Bayley, Obituary of Paul Rand, *Guardian*, 29 November 1996.
23. Otis Shepard, article in *Advertising Arts* magazine, New York, March 1931.
24. Quoted in Richard Hollis, *Graphic Design – a concise history*, Thames & Hudson (London), 1994.
25. John Bilney, promotional piece for Mediacom (Toronto), 1994.
26. Percy V Bradshaw, *Art in Advertising*, The Press Art School (London), 1928.
27. J Biegeleisen, *Poster Design*, Greenberg (New York), 1945.
28. Raymond Savignac, contribution to Pascal Courault and François Bertin, *Émail et Pub*, Editions Ouest – (Rennes, France), 1994.
29. Paul Rand, *Thoughts on Design*, Wittenborn & Company (New York), 1947.
30. Hiatt, *op cit*.

Advertising develops
1. Nathaniel Fowler, quoted in Victor Margoli, Ira Brichta, Vivian Brichta, *The Promise and the Product – 200 years of American advertising posters*, Macmillan (New York), 1977.
2. John E Kennedy, quoted in S Watson Dunn, *Advertising its role in modern marketing*, Holt, Rinehart & Winston (New York), 1961.
3. Samuel Johnson, *The Idler*, no 40, 20 January 1759.
4. John Barmas, 'Posters gave Bovril all-the-year-round sales', *The Poster*, October 1938.
5. '…the concept of brand image, which I popularised in 1953, was not really new; Claude Hopkins had described it twenty years before.' David Ogilvy, *op cit*.
6. W Teignmouth Shore, *Saturday Review*, 1907.
7. Henri Mouron, *op cit*.
8. Dick Dooijes and Pieter Brattinger, *op cit*.
9. Holst, in *De Bedrijfsreclame*, quoted by Dooijes and Brattinga, *op cit*.
10. Hahn, Ibid.

Poster rules
1. Oliver Green, *Art for the London Underground*, Studio Vista (London), 1990.
2. Abram Games, *Over my Shoulder*, Studio Books (London), 1960.
3. Walter Shaw Sparrow, *Advertising and British Art*, John Lane the Bodley Head (London), 1924.
4. WG Raffé, *Poster Design*, Chapman & Hall (London), 1929.
5. Bernard Villemot, quoted in Marie Bertherat, Veronique Gil, Elisabeth Kaplan, François Ekchojzar, *100 Ans de Pub*, Editions Atlas SA (Paris), 1994.
6. Raymond Savignac, quoted in Marie Bertherat, *op cit*.

7. Martin Hardie and Arthur K Sabin, *War Posters*, A & C Black (London), 1920.
8. Kyösti Varis, *Both Sides of Posters*, (Helsinki), 1996.
9. Ladislav Satnar, contribution to W H Allner, *Posters*, Reinhold (New York), 1952.
10. WH Allner, *op cit*.
11. Martin Hardie and Arthur K Sabin, *op cit*.
12. Abram Games, *op cit*.
13. Kaj Hansson, contribution to *Affisch Boken 2*, Liberg & Co (Malmö), 1990.
14. CB Falls, poster artist quoted in *The Big Picture Show*, a training video produced by The Creative Business, London, for Gannett Outdoor, New York, 1981.
15. Joseph Addison, *Tatler*, 14 September 1710, quoted in T R Nevett, *Advertising in Britain*, History of Advertising Trust, Heinemann (London), 1982.
16. *1000 + Campaigns on RSL Signpost database*, Research Services Ltd, 1996.
17. André François, contribution to WH Allner, *op cit*.
18. Georges-Louis de Buffon, *Discours sur le style*, address to the Academie Française, 1753.
19. And if you anagrammatically rearrange the letters of those three words to form two others … then the lesson will be reinforced.
20. Paul Rand, contribution to WH Allner, *op cit*.
21. Doug Linton, chairman of Ambrose, Carr, Linton, Carroll, Inc, speaking at Billi awards, Toronto, 1988.
22. Manfred Reiss, contribution to WH Allner, *op cit*.

The creative challenge
1. Kenneth Grange, in conversation with the author.
2. Raymond Savignac, contribution to WH Allner *op cit*.
3. Quoted in interview with Anthon Beeke, *op cit*.
4. Jeremy Bullmore, in conversation with the author.
5. Adolphe Mouron Cassandre quoted in Josef and Shizuko Muller Brockmann, *History of the Poster*, ABC Verlag (Zurich), 1971.
6. Raymond Savignac, contribution to WH Allner, *op cit*.
7. Erik Bruun, quoted by Kyösti Varis, *Both Sides of Posters*, (Helsinki), 1996.
8. Dave Trott, speaking at ITV conference, Monte Carlo, March 1991.
9. This became the title of a promotional piece by the contractor Mills & Allen.
10. Kyösti Varis, *op cit*.

11. Hans Hoffman, quoted by Ken Cato, article in *Affiche* No. 6.
12. RA Stephens, contribution to E McKnight-Kauffer, (ed), *The Art of the Poster*, Cecil Palmer (London), 1924.
13. Abram Games, *op cit*.
14. Voltaire in Arouet, Francois-Marie, *A Philosophical Dictionary: Poets*, 1764.
15. Alain Weill, in conversation with the author.
16. TS Eliot, *The Lovesong of J Alfred Prufrock, Collected Poems 1909–1963*, Faber & Faber (London), 1964.
17. William Shakespeare, *Hamlet*, act 2, scene ii.
18. Dorothy Parker, quoted by Alexander Woolcott, in *While Rome Burns*.
19. Quoted by Pat Schleger, in *Look beneath the surface*, a presentation on Hans Schleger at the Design Museum, London, 22 March 1990.
20. Hiatt, *op cit*.
21. Sammy Cahn, *I should care*, WH Allen (London), 1975.
22. Raymond Savignac, contribution to Pascal Courault, *op cit*.
23. Otis Shepard, *op cit*.
24. Milton Glaser, in *The Big Picture Show, op cit*.
25. Abram Games, *op cit*.

The strengths of outdoor
1. Phillips Russell, contribution to E McKnight Kauffer (ed), *op cit*.
2. W S Rogers, *A Book of the Poster*, Greening & Company (London), 1901, quoted by Alain Weill, *L'Affiche dans le Monde*, Avenir, Paris, 1984.
3. Article in *The Poster*, July 1938.
4. Francis Harmer Brown, *Campaign* magazine, 11 May 1979.
5. Jean-Luc Décaux, in conversation with the author.
6. Quoted by Lord Heyworth in an address at Unilever AGM, 1958.
7. Christopher Bagley and Andrew Morley, *Street Jewellery – a history of enamel signs*, New Cavendish Books (London), 1978.

Images and words
1. Abram Games, *op cit*.
2. Millais fils, *Life and letters of Sir John Millais*, quoted in Victor Margolin, *op cit*.
3. Masataka Ogawa, 'The History of Japanese Posters', in *Best 100 Japanese Posters 1945–89*, catalogue for 90th anniversary of Toppan Printing Company Ltd (Tokyo), 1990.
4. John Barnicoat, *Posters – a concise history*, Thames & Hudson (London), 1972.
5. Paul Rand, contribution to WH Allner *op cit*.
6 Raymond Savignac, contribution to

WH Allner, *op cit*.
7 'L'expression graphique de l'idée', Jean Carlu, quoted in Alain Weill, *op cit*.
8 Solved the anagram yet?*
9 Maiko Saito, interviewed in Bertrand Raison and Philippe Benoit, *Posters in Tokyo*, Nathan (Paris), 1989.
10 Abram Games, *op cit*.
11 Takashi Nakahata, interviewed in Raison and Benoit, *op cit*.
12 *Ibid*.
13 Abram Games, in conversation with the author.
14 Cassandre, quoted by Alain Weill, *op cit*.
15 Cassandre, quoted in *The Poster*, April, London, 1938.
16 Savignac, contribution to WH Allner, *op cit*.
17 Milton Glaser, contribution to *A Smile in the Mind*, Beryl McAlhone and David Stuart, Phaidon (London), 1996.
18 Paul Rand, *op cit*.
19 Abram Games, contribution to WH Allner, *op cit*.
20 Jan Morris, speaking on *The Holiday Programme*, BBC Radio 4, December, 1996.
21 'Name the greatest of all inventors. Accident.' Mark Twain, *Notebook*, 1935.
22 Louis Pasteur, address given on the inauguration of the Faculty of Science, University of Lille, 7 December 1854: in R Vallery-Radot, *La Vie de Pasteur*, Paris, 1900.
23 Alan Fletcher, *Beware Wet Paint*, Phaidon (London), 1996.
24 John Keats, *Ode on a Grecian Urn*, 1820.
25 Trevor Beattie, 'Getting Noticed', speech to Maximedia poster conference, Helsinki, 21 May 1996.
26 Aline E Louchheim, 'Posters: Challenge to the Artist', *New York Times*, 9 March 1953, quoted in WH Allner, *op cit*.

Brand and consumer
1 Judie Lannon, *What is postmodernism and what does it have to do with brands?*, The Journal of Brand Management, Volume 4, no 2, 1996.
2 Quoted in 'Brands v. Private Labels: Fighting to win', John A Quelch and David Harding, *Harvard Business Review*, January, February 1996.
3 Mary Goodyear, *The Postmodern Consumer*, speech at national conference of the Market Research Society of Australia, Sydney, 1994.
4 Stephen King, *Practical Progress from a Theory of Advertisements*, Admap vii(10), October 1975. Quoted in Colin McDonald, *How Advertising works*, The Advertising Association/

Bibliography

NTC Publications Ltd (Henley), 1992.
5 Winston Fletcher, *A glittering haze – strategic advertising in the 1990s*, NTC Publications Ltd (Henley), 1992.
6 Raymond Savignac, quoted in Attilio Rossi, *op cit*.
7 Kyösti Varis, *op cit*.

Beyond the billboard
1 Terry R Nevett, *Advertising in Britain*, History of Advertising Trust, Heinemann (London), 1982.
2 Reader's letter in *The Times*, April 1846, quoted by Nevett, *op cit*.
3 John Scorah, Adshel, part of the More Group, writing in *Brand Leader*, internal magazine of Unilever, Winter 1996.
4 Research quoted by John Scorah, *op cit*.
5 *Marketing*, 12 December 1996.
6 Ibid.

The future
1 Heinz Edelman, Preface, *Graphis Posters 75*, edited by Walter Herdeg, Graphis Press (Zurich), 1975.
2 David Gentleman, Obituary of Abram Games, *Guardian*, 29 August 1996.
3 Kazumaja Nagai, *Creative Works of Shiseido*, Kyruryudo (Tokyo), 1985.
4 Cassandre, quoted by Amos Stone, article *Advertising Arts*, New York, July 1931.
5 Tony Brignull, quoted in promotional booklet for Maiden, 1996.
6 Catherine Pepnister, 'Big title, big pay, no desk', *The Independent on Sunday*, 23 March 1997.
7 J William Wardell (former vice-president Gannett Outdoor), General Electric Capital Corporation, in conversation with the author.
8 Francis Goodwin, in conversation with the author.
9 Ian Forth, *Communicating in a postmodern world, Brand Leader*, internal magazine of Unilever, Summer 1997.
10 Ian Forth, *op cit*.
11 Judie Lannon, *op cit*.
12 Paul Feyerabend, *Science in a Free Society*, NLB (London), 1978.
13 Richard Holloway, director UK Outdoor Advertising Association, interview, *Guardian*, 28 October 1966.
14 Diane Cimine, Executive vice-president, Outdoor Advertising Association of America Inc, in conversation with the author.
15 Jean-Luc Décaux.
16 Pete Riordan, vice-president BBDO, New York, interviewed in *MQ* magazine, 18 September 1995.
17 John Hegarty, quoted in promotional booklet for Maiden, 1996.
* Anagram solution: David Bernstein

Further reading
25 Jahre, Art Directors' Club of Germany (Dusseldorf), 1989.
50 Years: Swiss Posters, selected by the Federal Department of Home Affairs (Switzerland), 1991.
Affisch Boken, Liberg (Malmo), 1990.
WH Allner, *Posters*, Reinhold (New York), 1952.
Stanley Appelbaum (ed), *The Complete 'Masters of the Poster'*, Eng trans, Dover (New York), 1990.
William F Arens and Courtland L Bovée, *Contemporary Advertising*, Irwin (Burr Ridge, Illinois), 1994.
Christopher Bagley and Andrew Morley, *Street Jewellery*, New Cavendish (London), 1978.
John Barnicoat, *Posters, A concise history*, Thames & Hudson (London), 1972.
Marie Bertherat, Véronique Girard, Elisabeth Kaplan and François Ekchajzer, *100 Ans de Pub*, Editions Atlas SA (Paris), 1994.
Daniel J Boorstin, *The Creators*, Random House (New York), 1992.
Edward Booth-Clibborn and Danielle Baroni, *The Language of Graphics*, Thames & Hudson (London), 1980.
P Courault and F Bertin, *Email et Pub*, Editions Ouest France (Rennes), 1994.
P van Dam, *A Century of Poster Art*, Netherlands Reclamenmuseum (Amsterdam), 1987.
Olivier Darmon, Rémi Noël and Eric Holden, *30 ans de publicité Volkswagen*, Hoëbeke (Paris), 1993.
Dick Dooijes and Peter Brattinger, *A History of the Netherlands Poster*, Scheltema & Holkema (Amsterdam), 1968.
Een Eeuw Affiche Kunst (A Century of Poster Art), Het Nederlands Reclamenmuseum (Amsterdam), 1987.
Winston Fletcher, *A Glittering Haze, Strategic Advertising in the 1990s*, NTC Publications (Henley), 1992.
Jan Fraser, *The American Billboard 100 years*, Harry N Abrams (New York), 1991.
Abram Games, *Over my Shoulder*, Studio Books (London), 1960.
Martin Hardie and Arthur K Sabin, *War Posters*, A & C Black (London), 1920.
Charles Harrison and Paul Wood, *Art in Theory: 1900–1990, An anthology of changing ideas*, Blackwell (Oxford), 1992.
Tim Healey, *Unforgettable Ads*, Reader's Digest (London), 1992.
Steven Heller and Seymour Chwast, *Graphic style: From Victorian to Post Modern*, Thames & Hudson (London), 1988.
Sally Henderson and Robert London, *Billboard Art*, Chronicle Books (San Francisco).

Walter Herdeg (ed), *Graphis Posters 75*, Graphis Press (Zurich), 1975.
Bevis Hillier, *History of the Poster*, 1969.
Diana and Geoffrey Hindley, *Advertising in Victorian England 1837–1910*, Wayland (London), 1972.
Richard Hollis, *Graphic Design – a concise history*, Thames & Hudson (London), 1994.
Bryan Holme, *Advertising, Reflections of A Century*, Heinemann (London), 1982.
Joseph Kroutvor, *The Street's Message*, Comet (Prague), 1991.
Alan and Isobella Livingston, *Encyclopedia of Graphic Design and Designers*, Thames & Hudson (London), 1992.
Victor Margolin, Ira Brichta and Vivian Brichta, *The Promise and the Product, 200 years of American Advertising Posters*, Macmillan (New York), 1977.
Colin McDonald, *How Advertising Works*, Advertising Association, NTC Publications (Henley), 1992.
E McKnight Kauffer (ed), *The Art of the Poster*, Cecil Palmer (London), 1924.
Luigi Menagazzi, *Manifesti Italiani*, Electa (Milan), 1988.
Rob Morris and Richard Watson, *The World's 100 Best Posters*, Open Eye Publishing (Horsham, West Sussex), 1993.
Fernand Mourlot, *20th Century Posters*, Wellfleet (Secaucus, NJ), 1989.
Joseph and Shizuko Muller-Brockman, *History of the Poster*, ABC Verlag (Zurich), 1971.
Kazumaja Nagai, *Creative Works of Shiseido*, Kyruryudo (Tokyo), 1985.
Terry Nevett, *Advertising in Britain*, History of Advertising Trust, Heinemann (London), 1982.
Robert Opie, *Rule Britannia*, Penguin (Harmondsworth), 1985.
Frank Presbery, *The History and Development of Advertising*, Doubleday (New York), 1929.
La Publicidad en el diserio urban, Publivia SAE (Spain), 1988.
W G Raffé, *Poster Design*, Chapman & Hall (London), 1929.
Bertrand Raison and Philippe Benoit, *Posters in Tokyo*, Nathan (Paris), 1989.
Nigel Rees, *Slogans*, George Allen & Unwin (London), 1982.
Maurice Rickards, *Turn of the Century Posters*, Evelyn, Adams and Maclay, (London), 1968.
Attilio Rossi, *Posters*, Hamlyn (London), 1969.
Ruedi Ruegg (ed), *Swiss Posters 1970–1980*, Seibundo Shinkosha (Tokyo), 1982.
The Shell Poster Book, with an introduction by David Bernstein,

Hamish Hamilton (London), 1992.
'That's Shell, that is!', An exhibition of Shell advertising art, The Barbican, exhibition catalogue, Acanthus Press (Wellington), 1983.
Brian Sibley, *The Book of Guinness Advertising*, Guinness Superlatives (Enfield), 1985.
Nick and Tessa Souter, *Illustrator's Source Book – 1850 to the present day*, Macdonald Orbis (London), 1990.
W Shaw Sparrow, *Advertising & British Art*, John Lane, the Bodley Head (London), 1924.
Kyösti Varis, *Both Sides of Posters*, Erweko Painotuote (Finland), 1996.
Alain Weill, *L'Affiche dans le Monde*, Avenir (Paris), 1984.
Stuart Wrede, *The Modern Poster*, The Museum of Modern Art (New York), 1988.
Wei Yew (ed), *Gotcha, the Art of the Billboard*, Quon Editions (Alberta, Canada), 1990.
Wei Yew (ed), *Gotcha Twice, The Art of the Billboard 2*, Quon Editions (Alberta, Canada), 1992.

Close-ups of these images appear on: pp10/11 Street Art, Fosters Lager, UK, 1995, Agency: BMP DDB Needham; pp40/41 Manolo Prieto, Osborne Sherry and Brandy, Spain, 1956;pp66/67 Coca-Cola, USA, 1945; pp84/85 Trident, Switzerland, 1995; pp112/13 Disneyland Paris, UK, 1996, Agency: Ogilvy & Mather; pp128/29 Manuela Riva, Perrier, Switzerland, 1990, Agency: Marsden Lacher Studer AG;

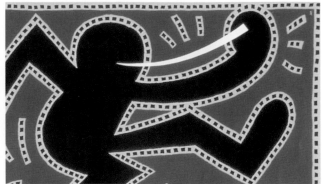

*pp156/57 Colgate, USA, 1989,
Agency: Young & Rubicam; pp176/77
Camel, USA, c1961; pp202/03
McDonalds, USA, 1980s, Agency:
McCann-Erickson.*

*pp220/21 KitKat, South Africa, 1994,
Agency: Ogilvy & Mather RS-TM;
pp228/29 Benetton, Italy, mid-1980s
to 1990s.*

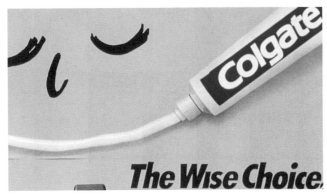

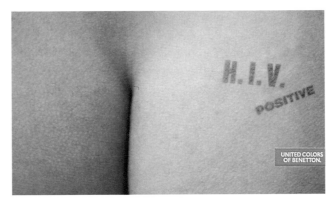

234 Acknowledgements

Susan for her ideas and insight.

Alain Weill for widening my horizons.

Pat Schleger for sharpening my focus.

David Jenkins and the team at Phaidon, especially my industrious editor Iona Baird and unflappable picture researcher Jemima Rellie.

Peter Kent, Roger Parry and the team at the More Group, especially Pierre Lasisz and Nan Huntingford.

Chris Dickens for contributing to the text. Dennis Sullivan for feats of discovery. Don Davidson for key suggestions.

Ann Blackwell and Lucy Bernstein for processing every word with good humour and imagination.

Finally, to colleagues at the Advertising Association, History of Advertising Trust, Outdoor Advertising Association of America, Victoria & Albert Museum and agencies, advertisers, media companies, consultancies, museums, archives, libraries and industry bodies around the world not all of whom, I fear, are listed here.

Raymond Ackah, Arno Adlivankin, Khamis Al-Muqla, Russell Gore-Andrews, Val A Arroco, Rex Audley, Trevor Beattie, Jan-Erik Berglund, John Bilney, Joseph R Blackstock, Jeremy Bullmore, Eric Burleton, James Carnegie-Brown, Diane Cimine, Andrew Cracknell, Michael Cudlipp, Tony Davidson, Chris Dickens, Paul Eastwood, Kyoshi Eguchi, John Ellery, Brian Gapes, Francis Goodwin, Kenneth Grange, Bahkeet al Hammad, Miguel de Heeckeren, John Hegarty, John Hope, KC Kam, Jennifer Laing, Cliff Lewis, Karl-Eric Linden, Doug Linton, Chris Lovelace, Brian McLean, Lisa Maxwell, Choe Nam-Suk, K Nicholson, Henry G Northcote, Colm O'Cuilleanain, Richard Orr, Geoffrey Probert, Peter Ralbarsky, Mario Reiner, Paul Rennie, Jonathan Riddell, John Ritchie, Florence Robert, Galina Savina, Paul Shearring, Margaret Timmers, Bill Wardell, John Webster

The first British poster. Frederick Walker, The Woman in White, UK, 1871.

Picture credits

Figures in italics refer to illustration captions.

This book has been produced with the help and support of the More Group, which, with its brands More O'Ferrall and Adshel, has been one of the leaders of the outdoor advertising industry for more than sixty years.

Phaidon Press Limited
Regent's Wharf
All Saints Street
London N1 9PA

First Published 1997
©1997 Phaidon Press Limited

ISBN 0 7148 3635 4

A CIP catalogue of this book is
available from the British Library

Printed in Hong Kong